Cyclops Wearing Flip-Flops

Cyclops Wearing Flip-Flops

THE BEST OF POETRY INSIDE OUT VOLUME VIII

EDITOR   *John Oliver Simon*

MANAGING EDITOR   *CJ Evans*

CONTRIBUTING EDITORS *Andrea Lingenfelter*
                     Martha Rutherford

EDITORIAL ASSISTANT *Audrey Larkin*

Cyclops Wearing Flip-Flops
The Best of Poetry Inside Out
No. 8

ISBN: 978-1-931883-18-4

Cover photos and book design by Ragina Johnson

Printed in Canada by Friesens Corporation

Distributed by The University of Washington Press

Rights to all translations published here revert to the translators unless otherwise noted.

   THE SAN FRANCISCO FOUNDATION
                                            The Community Foundation of the Bay Area

NATIONAL
ENDOWMENT
FOR THE ARTS

This project is supported in part by awards from the National Endowment for the Arts and The San Francisco Foundation, and charitable contribution from Amazon.com

Contents

V. Nuts and Bolts

Editor's Note

"We imagine words our own way!"
    Sydneé Blackwell, 6th grade

On a quiet afternoon in seventeenth-century Japan, a wandering poet sat by a pond. A frog leaped into its still and ancient waters with a splash, startling the nearby poet, who wrote:

古池や蛙飛び込む水の音
furu ike ya/ kawazu tobikomu / mizu no oto.

Four centuries later, on a foggy morning in 21st century California, elementary school students who don't know Japanese are reading and translating that famous haiku by Matsuo Basho:

Ancient pond alert
frog catapulting in pond,
sound of the water
    – Translated by Willie Qiu, 4th grade

Legendary pond!
frog fly into
sound of water
    – Translated by Jesús Fragoso, 5th grade

Which leads to the question: which of the following is the correct translation of *furu ike ya?*

> Ancient pond alert
> Legendary pond!

Standardized tests, whose preparation, results, and consequences dominate every aspect of the K-12 curriculum, suggest that every question has just one correct answer. This can cause immense anxiety in children that they might get the answer wrong. Translation, on the other hand, teaches that every problem may have a variety of interesting solutions. Children are empowered to seek divergent and creative possibilities, which better prepares them for the complexities of making real-world choices.

Translation and poetry combine to form a powerful synergy: translation is the deepest possible reading of a text and poetry packs a lot of meaning into a small amount of text. In the Poetry Inside Out program from the Center for the Art of Translation, students are given intriguing, accessible, and challenging work by some of the world's master poets, along with appropriate support, and learn to read poems over and over to themselves, chant them aloud, and examine each word as they translate. They end up reading each line up to fifteen times, while turning the structure and phrasing of their model "inside out" to create their own real, fresh, and deeply felt poems.

As kids begin to unpack what happens in a poem in the course of translating it, they become aware of complex verbal possibilities. Instructed by the poems they translate, they learn to apply figurative language to their own thoughts and feelings. The process of translating and then writing poetry builds connections, excites areas of neurons, and develops the muscle of the imagination. This sequence, repeated over sixteen sessions, greatly enriches students' language arts skills.

A Poetry Inside Out workshop is an extended apprenticeship in creative language with great poets—from Nobel laureates Pablo Neruda and Salvatore Quasimodo to classic figures like Ovid and Shakespeare. Sitting at the feet of these masters, PIO students learn how to create structure: building phrases into lines, lines into stanzas, haiku into collaborative renga, quatrains into sonnets and pantoums. Paradoxically, as they learn to work within the boundaries of poetic forms (be they traditional or innovative) students experience an eloquent and powerful explosion of imaginative creativity.

PIO brings Shakespeare, Ovid, Neruda, and Quasimodo into classrooms where 85% of the kids get free lunch. This work is based on acceleration rather than remediation—on high expectations for low-scoring students. Test scores notoriously follow income, but our belief is that poor kids are not less able to master complex subject matter, but are terminally bored by the pre-packaged, rote work they are being forced to ingest to prepare for standardized testing. Given something truly interesting to do all students will excel, debating at a high level in two or three languages about synonyms for a verb or learning a text so intimately that they can read it without looking at the page.

Poetry Inside Out began in the year 2000 by bringing the poetries of Spain and Latin America to Spanish bilingual and immersion classrooms. Now, PIO has extended the concept and practice of translation to work with poetry from across the world, having developed and field-tested a World Poetry Curriculum with poems written in a total of nineteen languages, as well as a Chinese PIO Curriculum with a full sequence of lessons for each of three levels—elementary, middle, and high school. Every classroom, regardless of its linguistic background, can participate in PIO through the World, the Chinese, or our traditional Spanish curriculum.

PIO runs a professional development program, with workshops around the country that prepare school staff to implement the PIO curriculum on their own. PIO also conducts poetry and translation workshops for museums, learning centers, and cultural institutions to complement their programs and exhibits.

As a Poetry Inside Out workshop draws to a close, the students also take their work out into the world, energetically revising their poems and translations, translating each other, then reading aloud to classmates, parents, and at public events. Finally, PIO students get to see their work published in a school anthology, which every child receives, and every two years, the most outstanding examples of their creative efforts are selected for this volume.

– John Oliver Simon
  Artistic Director
  Poetry Inside Out

Translation: The Way In

Translation: The Way In

Poetry Inside Out begins with a focus on translation itself. At first, the children translate relatively simple poems, which nevertheless focus their attention on word choice. Very quickly they learn that if they translate each word literally without being aware of its larger context, the result does not make sense. Students soon find that there are several alternatives to every translation. The Translator's Glossary on their Poem-Page (see the "Nuts and Bolts" section for in-depth descriptions of these terms) offers them synonyms galore, but each word has a slightly different shade of meaning. For example, the Spanish word *soledad* could be translated into English as either *solitude* or *loneliness*, with very different emotional connotations.

At the same time, the poems they are translating illustrate some very subtle lessons about poetry, which they absorb almost without realizing it. Poetry is written in lines, and the lines are grouped together into stanzas. The lines have a rhythm, which often sets up repetition and refrain that verges on chant or song. As the rhythm becomes more powerful, straightforward discourse is cloaked in the beauty of figurative language.

The five poems in this section reflect a palette of approaches to translating poetry. "Ciudad de cielo, a las cuatro" ("City of Sky at Four O'Clock"), by María Luisa

Artecona de Thompson (Paraguay, 1919–2003), is a good starting point, with straightforward repetition and refrain that are infused with passion and metaphor. "Ed è subito sera" ("And It Is Suddenly Evening"), by Salvatore Quasimodo (Italy, 1901–1968), is a first approach to translation from a language students may not have encountered before. The color poems of Rafael Alberti (Spain, 1902–1999) engage the senses and the visual imagination, while "Formas y colores de las palabras" ("Shapes and Colors of the Words") by David Huerta (Mexico, 1949–), treats words themselves as strange and luminous sensory objects. Finally, Xi Xi (Hong Kong, 1938–) takes us on a tiger hunt through a mountain landscape composed entirely of Chinese characters in "Striped Tiger in the Green Grass."

Session 1: For an Instant

"Ciudad de cielo, a las cuatro" ("City of Sky at Four O'Clock"), by prize-winning Paraguayan poet María Luisa Artecona de Thompson (1919–2003), is a good starting point for the Poetry Inside Out program. It is straightforward, with simple vocabulary and repetitive structure. It is not difficult for Spanish-speaking children to translate, nor is it impossible for non-Spanish speakers armed with a Translator's Glossary.

"Ciudad de cielo, a las cuatro" introduces metaphor at an elemental level, instructs in repetition and refrain, and above all, suggests that nuanced emotions and feelings can best be expressed in figurative language—using imagery to suggest a state of mind. "Ciudad de cielo, a las cuatro" encourages beginners to visualize, to invent, to establish a rhythm, and to vary on a theme. As they translate and imitate the poem, students are already well on their way toward becoming poets.

The class session begins by reading the poem aloud a number of times: the instructor reads aloud, the kids read a line or a stanza apiece, and the whole class functions as a poetry chorus. Then the class carefully goes over the Translator's Glossary before the students begin working in Translation Circles. The first time through, the aim is literal word-to-word correspondence. The second time through, the goal is to try to make it flow in English. Before the translation is done, the students will often write a paragraph explaining some of their choices in phrasing, or about what the poem might mean. For example, sixth-grader Alondra Cervantes wrote, "I think this poem is about her fantasies and her dreams of being successful. She is trying to say how it is at 4:00 in her city or country. 'I have a hard life. Maybe it's time for me to go. Different people go at different times. Life has ups and downs. You can't stop it.'"

Then—in a second instructional hour, if necessary—the class moves on to original poems patterned after the structure of "Ciudad de cielo, a las cuatro." The instructor provides a worksheet that enables the students to follow the structure of "Ciudad de cielo, a las cuatro" very closely, and yet each of the resulting poems is very different in tone. Of the poems collected here, Christina's is devoutly religious in spirit, Luana's guards a fierce independence, and Alexia's pushes fantasy to the limits.

Ciudad de cielo, a las cuatro

María Luisa Artecona de Thompson, Spanish (Paraguay)

Por un instante
yo soy de oro.
Por un instante
yo soy de plata.
Por un instante
yo soy de plomo.
Si el sol me besa.
Si el sol me llama.

Por un instante
yo soy de espuma.
Por un instante
yo soy de gasa.
Por un instante
soy de suspiros.
Si el sol me besa.
Si el sol me ama.

Por un instante
guardo en mi cuerpo
la mano ardiente
del sol de fuego,
o duermo quieta
junto a la luna
mientras la lluvia
me espera inquieta.

City of Sky at Four O'Clock

Translated by Yesenia Peña, 8th grade

For a moment
I'm of gold.
For a moment
I'm of silver.
For a moment
I'm of lead.
If the sun kisses me.
If the sun calls to me.

For a moment
I'm of bubbles.
For a moment
I'm of chiffon.
For a moment
I'm of sighs.
If the sun kisses me.
If the sun loves me.

For a moment
I save in my body
the glowing hand
of the fiery sun,
or I sleep calmly
close to the moon
while the rain
waits for me impatiently.

Original Student Poems

If I Am in Heaven

Cristina Ramírez, 6th grade

For a second
I am a careful angel
For a second
I am icy wings
For a second
soy de aire frío
If I am awake
If I am in heaven

For a week
I am of velvet feathers
For a moment
I am pale
For a week
I am soft bubbles
If I am awake
If I am in heaven

For a century
I keep in my wondrous eyes
The windy hand of God,
Or I sing peacefully
Beside the diamond fountain
While the white dove
soothingly lulls me to sleep.

Fuego y agua

Luana Cárdenas, 4th grade

Por un minuto, yo soy de fuego
Por un instante, yo soy de agua
Por un segundo, yo soy de nadie
Si me apagan, si me prenden

Por un momento, yo soy de aire
Por un momento, yo soy de tierra
Por un instante, yo soy de nadie
Si me dejan, si me libran

Por un segundo, guardo en mi memoria
el sueño olvidado o si pasa
junto al infierno mientras el cielo
me extraña inquieto

Fire and Water

Translated by the Author

For a minute, I am fire
For an instant, I am water
For a second, I am no one's
If they shut me down, if they turn me on

For a moment, I am air
For a moment, I am dirt
For a moment, I am no one's
If they leave me, if they free me

For a second, I save in my memory
the forgotten dream, if it passes
through the inferno while the sky
waits for me impatient.

Yo soy todo

Alexia L. Gómez, 6th grade

Por una semana,
soy invisible al ojo.
Por un mes,
¡soy rey de todo el mundo!
Por un segundo,
soy una flor tan frágil y rara.
¡Si las estrellas me protegen!
¡Si la luna me defiende!

Por un momento,
soy una fantasía encontrada
    en un libro de niños.
Por una hora,
soy un sueño que no se
    quiere ir.

Por un segundo,
soy el brillo del mundo con
    miedo de apagarse.
Si la gente cree en mí.
Si los corazones de los
    niños me aman.

Por siempre,
guardo en mis ojos,
el mundo de secretos;
o corro con esperanza,
junto al sol, mientras la
tierra
    del mundo
me jala con odio.

I Am Everything

Translated by Audrey Larkin

For a week,
I am invisible to the eye.
For a month,
I am king of the world!
For a second,
I am a flower, so fragile
    and rare.
If the stars protect me!
If the moon defends me!

For a moment,
I am a fantasy in a
    children's book
For an hour,
I am a dream that doesn't
    want to leave.

For a second,
I am the brightness of a
world that fears being
    turned off.
If people believe in me.
If children's hearts love me.

Forever,
I save in my eyes,
the world of secrets;
or I run with hope
next to the sun, while the
ground
    of the world
pulls me hatefully.

Session 2:
An Unknown Language

In the second session, the students translate "Ed é subito sera" ("And Suddenly It Is Evening") a brief, mysterious poem from a language few, if any, of them know: Italian. A complete Translator's Glossary makes this activity surprisingly easy, and Spanish-speakers will find a myriad of close cognates in this Romance-language text.

In this remarkable three-line poem, Salvatore Quasimodo (1901-1968) expresses the sense of solitude inherent in human existence as well as the brevity of our lives. The shape of the poem mirrors that of life: we arrive in the world alone; we briefly feel that we are at the center of things and are touched by a fleeting sense of joy and community; but happiness doesn't last and may even be an illusion. Suddenly darkness arrives, with a reminder of our mortality.

The verse follows a descending course in line-length and the number of syllables per line (twelve syllables, then ten, then seven). Quasimodo chose simple words, but arranged them with great care. He introduces a basic rhyme scheme ("*terra*" in the first line, "*sera*" in the third) and makes use of several rhetorical devices: metaphor ("*il cuore della terra*"); alliteration ("*sta solo sul*"); analogy ("*trafitto da un raggio di sole*"); and the final metaphor of evening as a symbol of death.

Having read aloud the strange sounds of approxi-
mated Italian and diligently looked up each word in the
glossary to create a draft of a translation, the students
are ready to make this poem their own. They start with
word association—replacing every important word in the
poem with another that has a similar meaning. What's another way of saying "ray?" *Beam. Laser! Fish!*—silliness
is a good first step on the way to poetic thinking, and as
the class throws out ideas, words open up and reveal their
mutability.

Ed è subito sera

Salvatore Quasimodo, Italian (Italy)

Ognuno sta solo sul cuor della terra
trafitto da un raggio di sole:
Ed è subito sera.

Everybody is alone on the heart of the earth
pierced by a beam of sun
it is all at once evening

— Alexus Smith, 5th grade

Translations

Todo el mundo está solo sobre el corazón
de la tierra
traspasado por un rayo de sol
y de súbito es el atardecer.

— Adilenne Torres, 4th grade

Adaptations

Everyone is lonely in the middle of the planet
stabbed by a beam of the star
and it is all at once dawn.

— Josephine Lee, 4th grade

Everybody is dancing in the field under the moon
doing the salsa dance thinking about
    their future with each other
and suddenly it started to rain

— Adapted by David Quintero, 5th grade

Anybody is lonely on the lungs of Jupiter
stabbed by a fish of star
and it is all at once dusk.

— Michael Ao Ieong, 4th grade

Session 3:
Coloring the Senses

There is a direct route between our senses and poetic expression, and "A la pintura" ("To Painting"), a group of brief poems about colors by Rafael Alberti (1902–1999), provide a foundation that enables students to use their growing poetic skills to sharpen their senses (and vice-versa). In three of these six poems, the color itself is the speaker, providing an example of personification. The other three poems are equally vivid evocations of a color, resonant with powerful nature imagery. These poems are very easy for Spanish-speakers to translate, and not difficult for non-Spanish speakers, given a complete Translator's Glossary. Six of the nine student-translators featured in this section don't even speak Spanish! In any case, the students' visual imaginations quickly go to work as they translate, and extend into their own original poems.

The lesson begins by listing colors *not* included in Alberti's six. Then students choose a color and brainstorm things and feelings associated with it. Students are encouraged to be extremely specific about the details associated with each color. Not just a Slurpee, but "the raspberry ice/ I got at Seven-Eleven." Not just money, but "the nickel, dime and quarter/ in the old lady's purse."

Color, so familiar and universal, is an easy way to get students to access their own experience as a source for poetry. The specificity of the task brings a sharpness of vision to the kids' work. Poetry doesn't have to be remote: it is one student's bedroom curtains, a baby brother's giggle, or a tree passed every morning on the way to school.

A la pintura

Rafael Alberti, Spanish (Spain)

Rojo

Soy el primer color de la mañana
y el último del día.

Red

I am the first color of the morning
and the last one of the day.

> — Translated by Saraí Castillo,
> 5th grade

Red

I am the first color of the morning
and the ultimate of the day.

> — Translated by Ethan Fox,
> 5th grade

Amarillo

Temo al azul porque me pone verde.

Yellow

I am scared of blue because it makes me green.

— Translated by Mariah Parham, 5th grade

I fear blue because it makes me jealous.

— Translated by Jason Aguirre, 4th grade

Blanco

Una línea, una letra
sobre mí. ¡Inolvidable maravilla!

White

A line, a letter
on me. Unforgettable wonder!

— Translated by Lakeviona Adams,
5th grade

Azul

Vénus, madre del mar de los azules.

Blue

Venus, mother of the sea of the blues.

— Translated by Diego Piceno, 4th grade

Negro

Un negro como flor de la alegría.

Black

A black like a flower of happiness.

> — Translated by Sulema Piceno,
> 3rd grade

Verde

Un verde sumergido en las aguas del tiempo.

Green

A green submerged in the waters of time.

> — Translated by Willie Qiu, 4th grade

Orange

The orange flower
fell down from
a tree like an angel
flying to heaven.

— Wesley Zhen, 5th grade

Purple

Purple violets growing
on a windy day
that float away
with the breeze
and the autumn.

— Stacy Hu, 4th grade

Turquoise

The good raspberry
ice I got
from Seven-Eleven
turquoise as blue
as the sky

— Iyanna Horace,
4th grade

Silver

Silver is like my heart
because when it stops
it turns into stone.

— Karen Arrellano, 3rd grade

Original
Poems

Brown

You stand under millions of leaves.

— Elaine Wen, 5th grade

Gray

School is gray
but I have wings
and slide right
in the mud.

— Keevan Tallon, 5th grade

Clear

Clear disappeared into a
glass window as it
blends into the wind.

— Ah'lia Parham, 3rd grade

Guess These Colors:

Juicy cherries bursting in my mouth
My blood pumping rapidly

— María Pedroza, 6th grade

The nickel, dime and quarter in
    the old lady's purse,
the crying girl's braces.

— Maya Primus, 5th grade

Session 4:
Words as Sensory Objects

Words become stale as we use them and write them over and over. They lose their flavor and turn into boilerplate. The poem "Formas y colores de las palabras" by David Huerta (1949–) gives very simple instructions on how to re-sensitize to language: pay attention to words as sensory objects; their sounds, their shapes, even their tastes and colors. "Any word has meaning," writes sixth-grader Alondra Cervantes, "only if the people who say it give it meaning."

Classroom teacher John Pluecker commented, "These exercises helped the students to understand that translation is only partially about 'meaning' and dictionaries. In fact, often what is more important is sound, structure, meter, rhyme, etc. Starting with these exercises forced the students to think in a different way—less analytically and more freely with an attention and a value placed on fun and creative solutions. These activities freed the students to see that praise would not come for being perfect or 'right,' but rather that we were looking for them to take chances, to think big and to take risks. This created better poetry in the end as well."

Of course, one problem with translating David Huerta's poem literally is that the English words don't have the same sound and flavor as their Spanish equivalents.

In English, "perfume" has two syllables, with the accent on the first blurred schwa-vowel, whereas in Spanish, *perfume* has *three* syllables, with the accent on the long, crooning u, which makes the word itself seem more fragrant.

Formas y colores de las palabras

David Huerta, Spanish (México)

Escucha una palabra con atención,
cualquier palabra.

Es puro sonido
pero algo
quiere decir:

naranja, una fruta; *avión*,
máquina que vuela; *Clodomiro*,
nombre de una persona; *Azucena*,
flor blanca.

Ahora vuelve a escucharlas
y encuéntrales
formas y colores:

¿no tiene *espada*
un saborcito metálico
muy adecuado?

Perfume con esa u
donde cae el acento
es profunda
y azul y verde.

Verónica tiene todas
las vocales, menos la u.

Carretera rechina
y serpentea.

Y así por el estilo…

Shapes and Colors of the Words

Translated by Sydneé Blackwell, 6th grade

Listen to the word with attention,
any word

It's pure sound
but it has something to say:

Orange, a fruit;
Airplane, a machine that flies;
Clodomiro, name of a person;
Lily, white flower.

Now come back to listen to them
and find forms and colors:

Doesn't a *sword* have
a very appropriate
metallic flavor?

Perfume with that u
where the accent falls
is profound
and blue and green.

Veronica has all
the vowels except "u."

The *road* grinds
and winds.

And like that because of the
style…

Forms and Sizes of my Life

Sydneé Blackwell, 6th grade

Listen to a word with attention
any word

It's just letters put together
but it has meaning

Samsung, a phone
Ferry, a boat
Barella, a name of a person
Falcon, a bird
Now stop, look, and listen
    to them
and find forms and sizes

Doesn't a *penny* have
a metallic flavor
very important, huh?

Cologne with that "O"
where the accent falls
is profound
and big and small

Song only has one
vowel, which is "O"

The *time* ticks
and tocks
and like that because
of the word

Sound and Words

Rosalina López, 6th grade

Listen to a word with focus and
your mind. Any word that drives
you to the limit.
It all sounds the same but look
deeper, what do you hear?

Black, a sad color but
    a happy one.
Car, a machine that drives.
Lionel, a name of a person.
Tulip, the name of a flower.

Now hear it again
and find color and objects
    in your mind.
What do you see?

Doesn't a *rose* have
    red petals?
Flower with that "ow."
Where the *ow* falls,
colorful and sweet.

Stars have only one vowel,
where are the rest?
The stars move, and more
    are coming
and never stop.

Escuche una frase

Alex Avalos, High School

Escuche una frase, con sensibilidad
una de su elección
vibraciones impecables
pero algo hay que decir
la vida es una fruta
que desafía todo
Alex, el nombre
Rosa, un ser poderoso
ver si usted oye
si se van a encontrar los colores
    de la vida
no tiene poder
un sabor diferente
es muy fresca
La vida sin "yo"
donde la verdad cae

es profunda
con diferentes colores
vence todos los vocales
excepción de la "U"
calles con mucho viento
y el miedo
sólo por el estilo

Listen to a Phrase

Translation by Audrey Larkin

Listen to a phrase
one of your choosing
impeccable vibrations
but with something to say
life is a fruit
that challenges everything
Alex, the name
Rosa, a powerful being
see if you hear
if they find the colors of life
it is without power
a different taste
it is very fresh
life without "me"
where truth falls

it is deep
with different colors
it defeats all the vowels,
"U" being the exception
streets full of wind
and fear
only due to style

Listen

Angel Calmo, 6th grade

Listen to the word
with close attention
it is saying a sound

Green, a land where trees grow
cars, mashing to go to places
roses, red flowers that are lovely to moms

Now come listen to beautiful poems
you will imagine how great it is
turn it to a sound and how your heart feels
feel it in a musical tone like hip-hop in the
street

See the Earth green and blue
with white clouds

Session 5: Find the Tiger

In the poem "Striped Tiger in the Green Grass" (綠草叢中一斑斕老虎) by Xi Xi (西西) (1938–), students are introduced to concrete poetry. The poem highlights the visual qualities of Chinese characters and contains a visual joke—readers of Chinese hunt in vain for the characters for "tiger." They are surprised when they find the "tiger" the poet intended. Students who don't read much or any Chinese are surprised that the boldface "tiger" they spot (often very quickly) isn't actually a tiger, although it looks like one—it is the character for "king" (王).

The poem invites students to explore a dense woodland filled with grasses, many kinds of trees, and a variety of different insects. With a Translator's Glossary, students hunt first for all of the insects and then for all of the trees, using radicals as their guides. This playful poem is the first introduction to Chinese for some of the students, and because it's like *Where's Waldo* and doesn't require students to be familiar with Chinese grammar, it's a good point of entry for those who are not familiar with the language.

Whether or not students read Chinese, "Striped Tiger in the Green Grass" offers a new way to get into a text: not by sequential reading but by exploring in any direction. Like David Huerta's "Formas y colores de las palabras," it makes words into tangible objects. "Striped Tiger in the

Green Grass" asks serious questions in a lighthearted way: what is a poem, and what are the limits of poetry? Where does the written word end and the picture begin?

Once students have spent some time getting acquainted with Xi Xi's landscape of words, they receive worksheets in the form of a grid that has fewer spaces than the poem has words, which forces them to focus on what they find most important. Students may "translate" the poem word by word, image by image, or as a picture of the scene as they envision it.

綠草叢中一斑斕老虎

杉杉松　蝗栢　梧蝶　蟬　榆桐
艸艸花艸鴰艸木艸艸艸隺艸艸草艸鳶艸樹艸
艸木艸楊艸山岫林艸草艸蚤艸山艸狐艸鳥艸
艸艸艸蟲艸山岫岫山岫艸花岫艸木岫
艸山蟻艸蟀艸木艸蜢岫岫鳥岫蟲艸木艸
艸山蟻艸木艸樹艸**王**艸艸木艸蚓艸花艸
艸林艸艸木艸艸艸花艸艸鳥艸山艸蟀岫岫艸

Translator's Glossary

綠：green
草：grass
叢：clump, cluster
中：middle, center;
here used as a prep-
osition, inside, in.
一：one
斑斕：striped
老虎：tiger
杉：China fir
松：pine tree
蝗：locust, grasshopper
栢：cypress, cedar
梧：parasol tree
蝶：butterfly
蟬：cicada
榆：elm

桐：paulownia, tung
tree, phoenix tree
艸：grass
花：flower
鴿：pigeon, dove
木：tree
虺：poisonous snake or
reptile
鳶：kite, hawk
樹：tree
楊：poplar tree
山：mountain
岫：cave; mountain peak
林：forest, woods
蚤：flea
狐：fox
鳥：bird

蟲：worm
蟻：ant
蟀：cricket
蜢：grasshopper
王：king
蚓：earthworm

find 6 tigers

— Gordon Kong, 4th grade

— Wendy Liu, 5th grade

— Jason Zeng, 4th grade

Striped Tiger in the Green Grass

Translated by Andrea Chen, 5th Grade

China pine- grasshopper cypress parasol- butterfly cicada elm phoenix
  fir   tree   tree   tree

grass flower grass   pigeon tree poisonous grass hawk tree
                                      snake

grass tree poplar mountain cave forest flea fox bird
                tree

grass worm mountain cave mountain grass   flower grass tree

grass worm mountain cave mountain grass flower grass tree

grass mountain ant   cricket grasshopper cave bird worm tree

mountain cave tree tree   **KING** tree earthworm grass flower

forest grass tree grass flower bird mountain cricket cave

Building A House of Words

Building A House of Words

As the students begin to translate poems, and to write their own original poems based on what they translate, they begin to grasp and to explore the many possibilities of poetry. After five sessions or so, they are writing with more originality and less fear of "getting it wrong." At this point, the focus of the Poetry Inside Out program shifts to poetic structures.

While poetry is about imagination and self-expression, its practice involves working with structure. As students master simple and then increasingly complex structures, they gain confidence and fluency: the beginnings of a poetic voice. Poems are generally written in lines (units of breath) and stanzas (units of thought). PIO students are first introduced to the concept of stanzas with the quatrain, a unit of four lines. Emily Dickinson, one of America's greatest poets, generally wrote in quatrains. After fully understanding the quatrain, students move on to the haiku, a unit of three lines, which is more difficult due to its strict syllabic count, and the tanka, a unit of five lines, which takes off from the haiku.

In the poems in this section, Alfredo Espino (El Salvador, 1900–1928) uses two quatrains to create a bird's nest, a house for the heart, a house of song. "Lai bij vārdi, kam bij vārdi...," a traditional Latvian chant, also written in two quatrains, allows improvisation based on a language the class won't likely know. Matsuo Basho (Japan, 1644–

1694) makes an eternity out of the brief moment of a frog's jump, while Tarawa Machi (Japan, 1962–) speaks in an ironic voice as fresh as the students' own. Finally, Jorge Luján (Argentina/Mexico, 1943–) uses the alphabet to string a poem down the length of the page.

Session 6:
A Nest Built of Lines

The quatrain is a very simple poetic stanza with endless possibilities, which is used in the poetry of many languages. It is a good first step along the road to a structuring of thought, which permits true spontaneity. The quatrain is balanced and symmetrical; its foursquare solidity helps young poets to organize their thoughts, and the quatrain may be rhymed or unrhymed. Although relatively short, with just four lines, it is easier than its shorter cousin the haiku, which requires more forethought and concision. The first two lines of the quatrain often open a window, while the final two lines complete the picture. When used with care and increasing inspiration, the quatrain shines like the Southern Cross.

Sixth-grade translator Desha Harper, who does not speak Spanish, consulted her Spanish-speaking classmates as she composed her translation of "El nido" ("The Nest") by Alfredo Espino (1900–1928). Her classmate Vy Huynh, also a non-Spanish speaker, passionately defended her own translation of the third line of this poem:

Line three of 'El nido' should say, 'that the tree awakens with a musical chest' because it makes sense with the line before that says 'In the hole of a tree his morning nest.' Also, it supports the flow of the poem because it rhymes. Finally this helps me understand the meaning of the poem which I think is: when the birdy awakes he's happy.

El nido

Alfredo Espino, Spanish (El Salvador)

Es porque un pajarito de la montaña ha hecho,
en el hueco de un árbol su nido matinal,
que el árbol amanece con música en el pecho,
como que si tuviera corazón musical...

Si el dulce pajarito por entre el hueco asoma,
para beber rocío, para beber aroma,
el árbol de la sierra me da la sensación
de que se le ha salido, cantando, el corazón...

The Nest

Translated by Desha Harper, 6th Grade

Because a tiny bird from the mountain has made
in the hollow tree a morning nest
the tree wakes up with music in his chest
it is like he had a musical heart...

If the sweet tiny bird peeks through the hollow
to drink dew and to drink the smell,
the tree from the mountains gives me a feeling
that his heart has come out singing...

De los sabores

El mango amarillo y jugoso
escurriendo jugo en tu boca
como limón cayendo
al pescado caliente

Of the Flavors

The yellow and juicy mango
dripping juice in your mouth
like lemon dripping
on a hot fish

— Moisés Bello, 4th grade

Mi corazón

Mi corazón
tiene flor como
estrellas
de dragónof dragons

My heart

My heart
has flowers, like
stars
of dragons

— Angélica García, 4th grade

Inspired
Poems

Every Fluffy Star

Every fluffy star
in the sky
speaks Peace as
its first language.

— Andrea Chen, 5th grade

The Rain

The rain sounds like
puppets dancing on the
roof on the water
of life.

A dream of rain
locks me in my
imaginary world of
blue water.

— Randell Rodríguez,
4th grade

Question Us

Question us about
the morning discovery
of a waterfall
in a flower

— Gerardo González, 4th grade

Sonidos

un ángel queriendo dormir
toca tu puerta, tú roncando,
las vidas dormidas,
tus sueños cortados

Noises

An angel wanting to sleep
knocks at your door, you snoring,
the lives sleeping,
your dreams cut

— Diana Rodríguez, 4th grade

Lenguajes

aprendí
lenguajes de
madera
historias de cuarzo

Languages

I learned
languages of
wood
stories of quartz

— Brayan Ortega, 4th grade

Las nubes

Las nubes son
cuando estoy jugando,
muy mojadas,
como un océano volando.

Pescados callados,
ratas comiendo
un estudio abandonado
donde todo es callado.

Luces apagadas,
espacio entero,
calle vacía,
flores en enero.

Las nubes son
calladas en mis sueños,
flotando en el cielo,
un cuarto negro.

The Clouds

The clouds are
when I'm playing
very wet
like a flying ocean.

Silent fish
rats eating
an abandoned theater
where everything is silent.

Lights that are turned off,
entire space,
empty street,
flowers in January.

The clouds are
quiet in my dreams
floating in the sky
a black room.

Alejandro Prieto, 4th grade

Session 7:
Chanting the Unknown

"Lai bij vārdi kam bij vārdi" is a traditional oak-tree charm for staunching blood, translated for our sister publication, TWO LINES, by Bitite Vinklers. The poem is structured in two quatrains, rhyming *aabc//bbxc*. Its strongly thumping trochaic tetrameter rhythm (BAH-bah-BUM-pum, BAH-bah-BUM-pum) comes through when you read it aloud. Latvian is one of the oldest Indo-European languages, and its kinship to familiar tongues is obvious in two words in this text: *vārdi* means "words" and *trim* means "three."

The class starts this activity by reading out loud, without the glossary. Each line is practiced by the whole class reading chorally, and then line-by-line by volunteers. Students often get carried into the rhythm of the line—they begin quietly but end up hollering, carried along by the beat. Then they receive this partial Translators' Glossary, which translates just seven key words:

Translator's Glossary

čūska: *snake, serpent*
dzēla: *bee, wasp*
lapiņa: *leaf*
ozoliņu: *oak tree*
stipri: *strong, powerful*
trim: *three*
vārdi: *words*

The assignment is to use these given meanings and improvise the rest of an invented translation while faithfully following the structure of the poem. The translation begins with brainstorming the first line: now that we know *vardi* is "words," what could *lai bij* mean?

> Write the…
> Some small…
> Learn good…
> Eat the…
> Choose these…

Now the kids are ready to "translate" the rest of the poem on their own. Are the resulting texts translations or original poems? This phase of the children's work is called *adaptations*. They are really closer in spirit to original poems than they are translations, but they are reinforced by the structure and imagery of the original. These adaptations are a powerful step on the road to the children writing their own real poems.

"Lai bij vārdi, kam bij vārdi ..."

Anonymous, Latvian (Latvia)

Lai bij vārdi, kam bij vārdi,
Man pašam stipri vārdi:
Daugaviņu noturēju,
Mietu dūru vidiņā.
Trim kārtām jostu jozu
Ap resnaju ozoliņu:
Cirta čūska, dzēla bite,
Ne lapiņa nedrebēja.

Words of Power

Translated by Bitite Vinklers,
professional translator

Whoever else knows words,
I know words of power:
I can stop a mighty river,
pierce the middle with a staff.
I can wind a threefold band
round the mighty oak:
the snake can strike, the bee sting,
not a leaf will tremble.

The original function of the charms here was to protect from danger or evil. The first quatrain refers to charms for staunching blood. The second speaks of protecting something by encircling it—creating a closed boundary that can't be penetrated by a harmful exterior force. The oak tree in Latvian folklore appears both as a sacred tree and as a symbol for a man.

— Bitite Vinklers

Write the Words

Write the words, write the words
Very very invincible words
Dinosaurs going to Mr. Language,
Who are you? I don't know you.

Three pieces of crunchy walnuts
A retired oak-tree
Poisonous snake, bee bite
Old leaves on the ground.

— Abdul Tawil, 5th grade

Adaptations

Some Small Words

Some small words, some small words
I'll speak powerful words;
dragons taking a nap,
maybe they dream of fire.

Three kangaroos went crazy
and they hit the oak tree.
Our snake, wasps in the mouth
while the leaves were toppling all around him.

— Jesury Blanco, 5th grade

Learn Good Words

Learn good words, learn good words
Repeat the powerful words:
All the words born from nature,
Feel the strong breeze.

Three petals gently float
Sweet sap from an oak tree:
Rare bugs, a bee bites,
Not a single leaf disappears.

— Crystal Huang, 4th grade

Remember These Words

Remember these words, remember these words
people hear powerful words
like angels singing on Sunday morning
bringing peace from day to day

— Lakeviona Adams, 5th grade

Session 8: Flying Frog

Haiku is a deceptively simple form. In three short lines, a haiku sets a scene and then delivers a surprise. The third line usually expresses a new insight, an image or comment that sheds new light on the two opening lines. Traditional haiku have three lines, with a syllable count of 5-7-5. Haiku don't rhyme (except in Spanish), but the syllable count and the economy of language forces haiku poets to compose poems with highly concentrated meaning and images.

In "Furu ike ya," by Matsuo Basho 芭蕉松尾 (Japan, 1644–1694), the scene is set in line one on an old pond. A frog leaps, plunges, jumps, flies, or dives in the second line. Line three tells us there is the sound of water—but what exactly is the sound is left up to the individual reader.

The action moves from tranquil alertness to sudden action to the broken quiet of the water, the echoes of this burst of activity. After the kids write their first versions they are given a handout with many English translations of this haiku, at least 30 of which—including a limerick version—can be found on the internet.

Written Japanese is a mixture of three parallel writing systems: *hiragana*, *katakana*, and *kanji*. This unique combination reflects the history of how Japanese came to be written. For much of its history, the Japanese language was only spoken. It was not until the period of China's Tang dynasty (618–907), when Buddhist missionaries from China reached Japan's shores, that Japanese started to be written down.

At first, everything was written in kanji, or Chinese characters, but this approach wasn't ideal. The Chinese and Japanese languages aren't related, and a writing system developed for Chinese, a language without verb conjugations or plurals, and where most words have one or two syllables, was a poor fit for Japanese, with its long multi-syllable words and many verb endings. Over time Japanese speakers developed the *kana* alphabets, or syllabaries. These include katakana and hiragana. Hiragana is used, usually in combination with kanji, to write verb endings and particles, words that perform a grammatical function without having independent meaning of their own. The Basho poem Poetry Inside Out students translated is written in a mixture of kanji and hiragana. Take for example this line:

蛙飛び込む　　　*kawazu tobikomu*

蛙 kawazu ("frog") is written in kanji, as are the verb stems, 飛 to- ("fly") and 込 ko- ("enter"). The hiragana び (bi) and む (mu) are used to fill out the Japanese readings. In the following line, hiragana is used to write the particle の (pronounced no), which is used to indicate the relationship between the water 水 (mizu) and the sound 音 (oto).

Another wonderful haiku poet, Carmen Leñero (Mexico, 1951–), helps older students get to the traditional 5-7-

5 syllable count. Leñero collected a whole book of river haiku under the title *Río*. One of these reads simply:

> El viento
> es un río
> que sueña.

The students then do a literal translation:

> The wind
> is a river
> that dreams.

They are then told to stay with this idea as they write a 5-7-5 syllabic version. They need to add something that isn't in the original—perhaps put in an adjective or two or a rephrasing:

> The black scary wind
> is a powerful river
> that dreams blue water.

> — Adapted by Francisco Zamora, 5th grade

> The powerful breeze
> is a blue scary river
> that imagines light.

> — Adapted by Jannett Contreras, 5th grade

Often the high point of the Poetry Inside Out residency is the day the class goes outdoors to write haiku. They walk to an urban lake, with its reeds and water birds, or sit in a little park with gang-tagged picnic tables under cotton-woods. The students are given clear directives and geo-graphical limits—don't go past the play structure! Some-times the teacher will work one-on-one with a student who's having trouble transcribing the moment, and it is not uncommon for a fourth-grader to write fifteen haiku in an hour.

As it is developmentally easier to count words than syllables, students are often given a worksheet with three, five and three words in each line, which is a haiku variant developed by Jack Collom at Teachers & Writers Collab-orative (www.tw.org) in New York.

古池や
蛙飛び込む
水の音

Furu ike ya
kawazu tobikomu
mizu no oto

— Matsuo Basho 芭蕉

Translator's Glossary:
古：old
池：pond
蛙：frog
水：water
の：of; indicates
relationship of
possession or
modification.
音：sound
飛び込む: to fly into, dive,
plunge, jump
や：marker for attention; i.e.,
an exclamation point

Ancient pond alert
frog catapulting in pond,
sound of the water

— Translated by Willie Qiu, 4th grade

Legendary pond!
frog fly into
sound of water

— Translated by Jesús Fragoso, 5th grade

Original Poems

La noche carpintera
Si prende las cien estrellas
Con papel luminoso

The woodpecker night
Lights up a hundred stars
With luminous paper

— Estefanía Tafolla, 4th grade

Las margaritas
en el pasto, las estrellas
detrás esperando su turno

— Karen González, 4th grade

The daisies
in the grass, the stars
behind waiting their turn

— Translated by Diana Rodríguez, 4th grade

The green grass
going into my face like
fish into water

— Lizbet Sandoval, 5th grade

Who am I
am I a shadow creeping
or am I nothing?

— Sandra Zavala, 5th grade

in the twilight
the sun was a memory,
I don't remember

— Bexy Hernández, 5th grade

The rock is
a silent creature on the
grass. It's strong.

— John-Jon Pita, 3rd grade

●

Oxalis sour in my mouth
Gully underneath me
Hummingbirds fly through me

— Luz María Vásquez Aldaz, 6th grade

●

Dark shadow in the
tree dancing but the sun comes
and it vanishes

— Jenifer Lomelí, 5th grade

I'm going to
Take the world and start
With this jewelry store

— María Lujano, 4th grade

●

The children running to see
the hurtful bees in the oak-tree
minding their own beeswax

— Coresha Hunter, 5th grade

My Thoughts

The powerful breeze
is a blue scary river
that imagines light

Danger grabs you now
it is around the corners
why is it so mean

Rain pours down the sky
it swirls like a hurricane
a falling ocean

Seashells discover
a wonderland of water
beautiful like snow

Life is around you
it shivers as hard as a snake
you are what you are

— Jannett Contreras, 5th grade

Session 9:
Renga Round the World

The classic tanka adds two seven-syllable lines to the haiku's 5-7-5 syllable lines. Starting as early as the eighth century, Japanese poets began to compose collaborative series of tanka, which were known as *renga* (連歌 "linked verse"). One poet would begin with a haiku stanza, and a second poet would finish it off with two seven-syllable lines, and so on—back and forth or around a group. The PIO program continues this tradition in the classroom, using worksheets that pass from hand to hand. The first student writes three lines; the second student finishes off with the final two lines and then starts a new tanka before passing it on to the next person.

The act of collaboration eliminates self-critical anxiety. Coming in right in the middle of the poem, the second speaker can feel free to shoot off in a new direction or make an ironic, disjunctive comment, sparking spontaneity. One fifth-grade class generated over two hundred tanka in a single hour, many of them excellent, and all of them exciting to the participants, who laughed and cheered as the instructor read them aloud.

Tawara Machi's (俵万智) (1962–) tanka take full advantage of the diversity of written Japanese. Many of her poems incorporate kanji, hiragana, and katakana, which gives them a varied and interesting texture. This typographical richness mirrors the etymological richness of Japanese, with Chinese loan words or words the poet wants to highlight written in kanji, other foreign loan words in katakana, and the rest in hiragana. If English were written in a combination of fonts or alphabets that reflected the Latin, Greek, Germanic, and Celtic roots of various words, we would see a similarly complex mixture of symbols on the printed page.

子どもらが十円の夢買いに来る駄菓子屋
さんのラムネのみどり

Tanka

children come
to the candy store
to buy a 10-yen dream

green bottles
of lemon soda

— Translated by Juliet Winters Carpenter,
professional translator

niños vienen
a la tienda
para comprar un sueño de 10 yen

botellas verdes
de soda de limón

— Traducido por Allison Santiago, 8° grado

書き終えて切手を貼ればたちまちに返事
を待って時流れだす

I finish writing
stick the stamp on
and time begins to flow

toward the moment
of your answer

— Translated by Juliet Winters Carpenter

termino de escribir
pego el timbre
y el tiempo empieza a fluir

al momento
de tu respuesta

— Traducido por Uriel Bravo, 8º grado

恋をすることまさびしき十二月ジングルベルの届かぬ心

loneliness
of being in love
in December

my heart impervious
to "Jingle Bells."

— Translated by Juliet Winters Carpenter

soledad
de estar enamorada
en diciembre

mi corazón insensible
a "jingle bells"

— Traducido por Yésica Gutiérrez, 8° grado

誰からも忘れ去るれたような夜隣の部屋
に鳴りベルやまず

on a night
when the world
has forgotten me

the phone next door
rings on and on

— Translated by Juliet Winters Carpenter

en una noche
cuando el mundo
se ha olvidado de mí

el teléfono de a lado
suena y suena

— Traducido por Jessica García, 8º grado

I have a
dream that makes me think
am I me?

Down down down the cliff
gently down the big street

— Saraí Castillo & Luis Tejeda,
5th grade

Sunshine hits my
eyes my eyes burn when
the sun's bright

and the eyes go blind
to be born again inside

— Randell Rodríguez &
Jesús Fragoso, 5th grade

Original
Poems

I said no
No no no no no
To my mother

But my mother says yes
Yes yes yes yes yes

— Kathy Espinoza & Janiah Owens,
4th grade

A star shines
Like the sun in fire
Shiny sun star

It shines like luminous paper
Or glittery lipstick or window

— Karen Rodríguez & Estefania Tafolla,
4th grade

Milky Way is
A big galaxy so we
Are like dust

I don't understand it so
I am writing this poem

— Rigoberto Bañuelos & Karen
Rodríguez, 4th grade

corazón de hielo
dulce sabor dentro de mí
niño ya nacido

ojos negros como la noche
llorando por los besos de sus papás

heart of ice
sweet taste inside of me
baby boy barely born

eyes so black like the night
crying for his father's kisses

— Natalie Guzmán y Humberto Alcoser,
4th grade

Session 10: The Alphabet

Literary translation is a series of choices, and if the choices were obvious it would certainly make translation boring. But translating a poem is *never* boring. It's the wrestling with words, dancing with metaphors, and the sheer physicality of rendering a poem from its original language into another that entices students of Poetry Inside Out. PIO students are continuously making choices involving synonyms, form, cadence, structure, and much more.

In this session, PIO students are faced with the formidable task of translating a clever abecedarian poem by Argentine poet Jorge Luján (1943–), with some admirable results, like the rendering by eighth-grader Alexandría Pérez. It would have been challenging enough to concretely translate the content of this poem, but Alexandria also wanted to maintain its acrostic, abecedarian structure. At first, this proved difficult because she didn't recognize some of the words' meanings, but she began by translating the words she immediately recognized (like *felices, lluvia, mojando*) and those that instantly fit into the abecedarian, such as ark, gorilla, and parrots.

Next Alexandría chose to find English synonyms for as many of the Spanish words that she could then fold into the alphabetical form. For example *orondo*, which generally means "fat," she translated as *obese* for the "o" verse.

For *diluviar*, which is the verb "to pour," (as in "a pouring rain"), Alexandria chose "deluged" to fit for "d."

Then the eighth-grade translator made a pivotal choice—Luján's poem uses one-word lines, and in some cases Alexandría could not find one-word equivalents that could also fit the form. She decided that, when necessary, she would break from that form, finding it was more important to "keep the images." So for *ensenadas* (bay or cove) she envisioned an entrance, taking the creative liberty of describing it as a "Deluged/Entrance to the creek." "Felices/Gorilas" (Happy/Gorillas) became, "Full of joyful/Gorillas."

Abecedario

Jorge Luján, Spanish (Argentina)

Arca
Bienaventurada
Cruzando
Diluviales
Ensenadas,
Felices
Gorilas
Hamacándose
Indolentes,
Juntando
Kilogramos,
Luminosa
Lluvia
Mojando
Náuticos
Ñandúes,
Orondos

Papagayos
Que
Rezongan,
Solícitos
Tigres,
Unicornios
Valerosos,
Wapitíes,
Xilócopos,
Y
Zorros.

Alphabet

Translation by Alexandría Pérez, 8th grade

Ark,
Blessed,
Crossing the
Deluged
Entrance to the creek
Full of joyful
Gorillas
Having a lazy swing,
Indolently
Joining
Kilograms,
Luminous rain,
Much drenching of
Nautical rheas,
Obese
Parrots
Questioning,

Rumbling,
Solicitous
Tigers,
Unicorns so
Valiant,
Wapitis,
Xylocopa and
Young
Zen foxes

ABC Poem

Caroline María Woods-Mejía, 7th grade

Above the mango tree
Below the shiny moon and stars
Careful are the waves of the sea
Dirt and leaves begin to char
Endless nights seem to fade
Forgetting all thoughts and plans
God took my soul away
He left me here and scarred
    are my hands
I was all alone, the night so dark
Just me and nature, the trees
    so green
Killing the forest—nothing
    left but bark
Leaving me nowhere to be seen
Minute by minute and hour
    by hour

No one seems to pass by
Only the rain falls into a
    never-ending shower
People I don't know nod and say hi
Quietly I walk
Roaring are the tigers and animals
    in the jungle
Something invisible talks
Talking is useless I can only
    mumble
Under my umbrella I am semi-dry
Vision is blurred
Words that are meaningless
    seem to fly
Xibalbá is where I was lured
Y did I commit such a crime?
Zebras finally tell me why

Original
Poems

Youthful Zen

Alexandria Pérez, 8th grade

Awakened
By
Crying for the
Death of a tío.
Endless
Fear
Going crazy
Hear his voice
Inside me
Just
Kuz I
Leave out all the rest
Makes
Never-ending
Options for this
Psycho kid.
Questioning his

Return?
Sure
To
Unite with his soul.
Vicious
Wonder.
X-treme
Youthful
Zen.

My False Sun

Delia Silva Rodríguez, 8th grade

Always running
Before the handcuffs and the sirens
Caught between a wall and a wall
Drowning in the lies you told me
Everyone is
Falling
Grace that's not deserved
Hearing that shouldn't be heard
I'm inside the house where it happened
Jumping at the smallest sound
Killing me with the memories
Leaving me speechless with the words you told me
My mind can't produce thoughts
Never ending *crepúsculo*
Old faces appear
Promises you couldn't keep

Quivering at the false kindness you showed
Respect is earned not bought
Screaming at the thought of seeing you again though it's
Tough not to feel a little joy
Until you grovel on your knees I will forgive
Vicious flashbacks suffocate me
Wondering how long I've been holding my breath
X-ed out of reality
You left without a good excuse, your words leave scars
Zero thoughts

Where I'm From

Where I'm From

As students practice literary translation, while learning to use poetic structures inherited from many cultures across the centuries, they build a platform that enables them to express the many facets of who they are, where they come from, and the often dangerous, vulnerable world that surrounds them.

Poetry helps kids articulate the challenges they face, from the personal to the global. Poetry allows them to give voice to their impressions and beliefs in a way that is unlike any other outlet provided by their education. During the years when young people are working to figure out who they are, poetry provides them a voice for their unique identity.

The poems in this section, written in Spanish, French, Latin, and Tzotzil Maya, span two millenia. Haitian poet René Depestre (1926–) finds metaphorical identity as a river that washes away human suffering. Pablo Neruda (Chile, 1904–1973) observes a lizard, utilizing the poetic form of the ode as a window on the universe. From two thousand years ago, the Roman poet Ovid (42 BCE–17/18 CE) describes the chaos at the beginning of the universe, and contemporary Mayan poet Rominka Vet sees a dancing jaguar in the sky.

Self, society, and planet: in one order or another, the children take on these large subjects, and take them to heart.

Session 11: The River of Self

"I write poems," comments eighth-grader Delia Silva Rodríguez, "because it allows me to say things I don't have the guts to say out loud. To me, when I write a poem, I'm showing rather than telling. I like painting a picture in people's minds when they read my poems."

Translation, as a profound language process, reaches deep into students' hearts, and can stimulate profound meditation on the ageless themes of identity, self, and society. Haitian René Depestre's (1926–) poem "La rivière" provides a channel into this type of poetry of self-identity. The poem links the poet with both the natural world of the river flowing and the societal reality of people's suffering.

"La rivière" works as an extended simile. In an absolute metaphorical plunge, self becomes river. Depestre examines the idea of poet-as-river from every angle, considers all implications, and transcends his premise with the pledge to wash away all suffering. Students write poems that start with the words "Voilà, it's done. I have become…" and follow up their transformation by asking, as Depestre does, a series of questions.

La Rivière

René Depestre, French (Haiti)

Voilà. C'est fait : je suis devenu une rivière.
Ce sera une grande aventure jusqu'à la mer
quel nom me donnera-t-on sur les cartes ?
d'où vient ce cours d'eau inconnu ?
quel ciel reflète-t-il dans ses flots ?
quelle joie, quelle faim, quelle douleur ?

Pardonnez-moi messieurs les géographes
je n'ai pas fait exprès
j'aimais voir couler l'eau
sur toutes les soifs
il y tant d'assoiffés dans le monde
pour eux me voici changé en rivière.

Je n'aimais pas voir couler les larmes
étant rivière je pourrai qui sait ?
couler à leur place.

Je n'aimais pas voir verser le sang
étant rivière je pourrai
être versé à sa place.
Mon destin est peut-être d'emporter
à la mer toutes les peines !

The River

Translation by Anita Sagástegui, professional translator

Voilà. It's done: I have become a river.
This will be a great adventure to the sea
what name will they give me on the maps?
where did this course of unknown waters begin?
what sky does it reflect upon its streams?
what joy, what hunger, what pain?

My apologies to all geographers,
I didn't do this on purpose
I just loved to watch the water flow
upon all of the thirsts
there are so many thirsty people in the world
it is for them that I've become a river.

I never liked to see tears fall—
being a river, who knows?
perhaps I could fall instead.

I never liked to see blood pour—
being a river
I could be poured instead.
My destiny may then be to carry away
all suffering to the sea!

Butterfly

Voilà. It's done. I've become
a splendid butterfly.

My cocoon is wide open.
Will someone make me suffer?

Will I land on the most beautiful flower?

Will I make it back home?

My new wings take me everywhere
but this world is too big for me.

No one but myself
to wonder at this magnificent world.

— Anahí Medrano, 7th grade

Wind

It was not hard, it was not easy, but
I have become the wind.
I forge paths through rocky earth.
I am a powerful foe,
or a great friend.
I am unmatched
for I cannot be broken.
Not by land, nor by sea.
People run before me, scared and afraid.
but why do they run? For I shall not hurt them.
but if I am mad or sad, they should run from me,
for I will wreak havoc and chaos across the land.
Then I will return to my normal state.
Calmer than the clouds.
I am scared of what I've done.
So I hide never to be seen again.

— Lackana Sot, 6th grade

My World

I sketch trees, moss and clouds;
a flying bulb of light circles around me
comets of fire race toward the friend with
many open arms, greeting them
a bit of sunshine I spread on my cookie
comes from the golden lantern of pure sweetness
obscured in endless fields
of mother earth's carpet

I transform into the exhalation of God
blowing upon the dawn,
getting ready to cover the earth
in silvery white
a silent whisper prepared to attack
a child's fear, concealed in school, knocks anyone out,
for countless hours, waking up in a daze
a flash of light that comes for all my anger
zapping all I scorn

— Thong Dinh, 8th grade

Then

I was asleep
then I turned eight
then I turned into stone
then it was winter
then spring.

— Qwest Hewitt, 3rd grade

My Name

A dirty puddle.
Fear?
A simple flame. A
tiny definition. Una gota
en el cielo. A corner
of light.
A smooth lyric. I'm
one in a million. As unique
as a star and bright as
a burnt-out light bulb.
Mayra?
A book leading to heaven.
A ladder to infinity.
The password leading
to lost.
Why?
Why so cold & alone?
Answer. Because the
light in the sky
doesn't shine anymore
& the mother
cries day and night.
As you stare into your
deep mind trying
to make sense
of what you just
read.
You won't… because the
key is forgotten.

— Mayra Centeno Mendoza,
7th grade

Deep

Coming out strong
but being dipped in the disgrace
with an ocean full of sorrow
her heart a paper in the brain
not sure of what she is, and what
she knows
lying in her bed & her pillow
dunked in shame
dead within a sentence
her heart a shattered glass
not knowing what to do
lost in faith
a face in a clasp
still blooming
with drops of water
bombing
with fire
Dead
without color

— Esmeralda Avila Torres, 7th grade

Obsidian

You, who are the widened pupil
Of a scared eye in the dark.

Compressed night,
Ragged blanket that sometimes
Covers the bleached moon,
Coffee over which the stars converse.

You, who were there before water,
Before air,
Before life.
Before time could wrinkle and
     pucker your face,
And touch your eye with ugliness of age.

You who, accompanied by turkey feathers,
Hung from the ear

And tipped the weary arrows
Of a proud, godly chieftain,
As he boldly struck down the barrier
Between sound and love.

You, who are the mole,
That burrows eternally through
The warm, deep dirt;
The soul of the earth,
Disguised as wealth.

You are the only beauty
That endures.

— Deedee Pearce, 8th grade

My Hero

My father
A book that has its secret
He has awakened me from my dreams

When I am sad he lifts me up
from the cloud that is on me

When I am in need he comes
to the rescue and saves the day

Me and my dad are the stars
that depend on each other

Then when the time comes he lets me
out of the nest into the gracing air

At the last moment a tear comes down
off my cheek
when he passed on
he moved to watch me from the sky

— José Arciga, 6th grade

Session 12:
Children of Children

African-American poet Oscar Brown Jr. (1926–1995) wrote:

> The children of children
> Cry out every day
> They beg you for rescue
> And what do you say?

The children of children that Poetry Inside Out reaches every day in the classroom are begging for a kind of rescue: from low expectations and remedial curriculum. Often, they have been forced to deal with migrations across borders and cultures that have not always been advantageous for them:

> Soy de aquí
> y soy de allá
> from here
> and from there
>   – Gina Valdés

In this poem, "Where You From?", Chicana Poet Gina Valdés (1943–) uses code-switching, going back and forth between Spanish and English, writing in Spanglish, to express her double identity as a Latina American, a situation shared by millions of children in the United States. Even though she is not a native Spanish speaker, this poem spoke to sixth-grader Desha Harper, who translates a portion of the poem (English to Spanish and Spanish to English) as:

I am from south
and from north
raised mix-upped
and off-track
crossing bor-
ders cruzando

Creo que el mundo es bello,
que la poesía es como el pan, de todos.

I believe the world is beautiful,
and that poetry, like bread, is for everyone
    – Translated by Jack Hirschman

Some of the best poets in history were forced to take difficult stands on principle. Nazim Hikmet was imprisoned for years, and though he finally escaped into exile, he could never go home to his beloved Turkey. Pablo Neruda once escaped from his native Chile on horseback across a mountain pass. Roque Dalton of El Salvador, who gave his life to the struggle, but was ironically killed by his own supposed comrades, wrote:

These poems are powerful models of expression for kids who feel "off-tracked" and "mix-upped" in a world that does not always seem fair to them, a world where bilingualism is often viewed as a handicap instead of a double capability, where they may have to deal with racism, poverty, and gangs. The PIO program allows children the expressive space in which to confront these very real challenges.

I am

Isis Delgadillo, 6th grade

I am from here
and from all over there
de aquí y de allá
nacida en Oakland
born in Oakland
raised by my parents
yo fuí criada de mis padres
mi boca todavía
sabe de love
with cariño
but I get angry
cuando my parents don't love me
when I look at my dad's eyes
se ven que me tienen amor
mi nombre es Isis
my name is Isis

se escucha
it sounds like
a refreshing wind
because it goes
like I-sss-i-ss
cuando se escucha it sounds like
I-ss-i-ss como el viento
que me refresca en la
mañanita cuando veo la
sonrisita de mis padres
pero yo creo
but I think
when I don't
see my parents
for a long time
todavía voy a

recordar la sonrisita
en la mañanita
para siempre
y la miradita
en los ojos
de mamá, papá
de amor
with love.

Where You From?

Lackana Sot, 6th grade

I've been reading some poems
these people were from different places
and it has got me wondering:
where am I from?
I know I'm from Cambodia
but let's get spiritual.
My heart is of solid gold.
My blood beats for the sound of happiness.
I am the sky, loving to see new places.
I am the ground, traveling far distances.
I am the sea, surrounding land.
I am the air, surrounding the world.
I am the fire that burns in my soul.
I am…
I am…
I am the world.

Puente

Hay tantas fronteras
separando mi hermano
que no podemos imaginar
pero existe un puente
para hacerlo sonreír

Bridge

There are so many borders
separating my brother
that we can't imagine
but there is a bridge
that has him smiling

— Angélica Rodríguez, 6th grade

Oakland

Chaos at the Oakland
Coliseum waiting
for the Raiders
to win
Starving watching
people eat
their chicken wings
with a cold soda
I eat the leftovers
from the kitchen stove

— José Luis Moreno, 6th grade

Crying

I never cry
on my birthday
but I sometimes cry
when my Dad leaves
to Mexico

— Gaby Martínez, 3rd grade

My Language

When I speak English
I feel as if I don't belong
    a grain of rice
    in a jar of beans

Speaking Spanish
es mi idioma número uno
    Spanish is an
    idioma hermoso

When
yo hablo español
    I feel
    mariposas coming out of my mouth

Yo amo mi idioma número uno

— Jessica García, 8th grade

Homeless

Cold, old, homeless
no home an unfuzzy coat
says "God bless"

— Tobias Goodwin, 3rd grade

My Hood

My 'hood is stupid
calling themselves red or blue
what's the point?
Killing innocent people
dying for red or blue
what's the point?

— Alexandra Ramírez, 6th grade

En mi sangre

The rhythm of Oakland
runs through my blood
   through my blood
   through my blood

The rhythm of Oakland
drums everyday
   in my mind
   in my mind

The rhythm of the killings
beats in my heart
   in my heart
   in my heart

— Jorge Escamilla, 8th grade

Session 13: Dancing Jaguar

The Maya established one of the great civilizations of the ancient world, building enormous temples and cities, developing a written language, and making intricate astronomical calculations. Today, there are 23 Mayan languages, which are spoken by millions of people in southern Mexico and Guatemala.

In the PIO classroom, the ordinary process of translation is reversed with this poem. First, the students are given the original poem in Tzotzil; and after reading the poem aloud, we supply its translations in Spanish and English, along with a Translator's Glossary in which each Tzotzil word is followed by a blank. Students must reason backward from the translations to figure out the meaning of each word in the original.

When "Bolom Chon" was presented in a workshop for adults at the Chabot Space & Science Center in Oakland, California, the participants were quick to protest that they were not poets. But as they translated the Maya Tzotzil and wrote their own poems, they fell into the sonorous rhythms of both English and Spanish. Classroom Assistant Molly Wheeler commented: "as they translated and wrote their own poems their words took on a kind of celestial gravity. We heard it in their voices as they read aloud. The word darkness, said with solemnity, becomes many things…"

Bolom Chon

Rominka Vet, Maya Tzotzil (Mexico)

Bolom Chon ta vinajel.
Bolom Chon ta Banumil.

Yajvalel ta vinajel.
Yajvalel ta Banumil.

Koxkox avakan, Bolom Chon.
Natik avakan, Bolon Chon.

Tinitin avisim, Bolom Chon.
Natik avisim, Bolom Chon.

Likan, tot.
Likan, me.'

Va'alan, tot,
Va'alan, me.'

Totzan, tot.
Totzan, me.'

Jk'upintik ta Banumil.
Jk'upintik ta vinajel.

Tigre que baila

Translation by Ambar Past, professional translator

Tigre que baila en el cielo.
Tigre que baila en la Tierra.

Guardador del cielo.
Guardador de la Tierra.

Tienes cojita tu pata, Tigre que Baila.
Tienes larga tu pata, Tigre que Baila.

Peluda tu barba, Tigre que Baila.
Larga tu barba, Tigre que Baila.

Levántate, papá.
Levántate, mamá.

Párate, papá.
Párate, mamá.

Súbete, papá.
Súbete, mamá.

Nos gustamos aquí en la Tierra.
Nos enamoramos aquí en el cielo.

The *Bolom Chon*

Translated by Ambar Past

Dancing Tiger in the sky.
Dancing Tiger on the Earth.

Keeper of the sky.
Keeper of the Earth.

You have a limp, Dancing Tiger.
You have a long foot, *Bolom Chon*.

Your beard is fluffy, Dancing Tiger.
Your beard is long, *Bolom Chon*.

Rise up, Father.
Rise up, Mother.

Stand tall, Papa.
Stand tall, Mama.

Step up, Papa.
Climb on, Mama.

We like each other on the Earth.
We fall in love here in the sky.

In 28 Days

Mireya Casarez, community member

In darkness you come

Filling the sky with your warmth
Filling me with your energy
You bring the memories of the
    grandmothers

In darkness you come
Filling weakness with strength
Filling sorrow with Joy

You bring the wisdom of the ancestors

In darkness you come
Filling the distance between us
Filling the emptiness with light

You bring the faith of the believers
You trade into light

In darkness you come

Original
Poems

Ojos de la noche

Martha León-Miakhail, community member

Ojos de la noche
que miran sobre mí

Ojos de la noche
que mis sueños cuidan

Luna sobre la tierra,
que cuidas mis sueños

Luna sobre la tierra
de pronto será día

Mira que ya amanecí
la mañana pronto estará aquí

Mira que ya amanecí
la vida hay que vivir

Eyes of the Night

Translation by John Oliver Simon

Eyes of the night
that watch over me

Eyes of the night
that protect my dreams

Moon above the earth,
protecting my dreams

Moon above the earth
soon it will be day

Look, it is dawn
soon it will be morning

Look, I have awakened
life must be lived

Session 14:
Chaos in the Universe

Two thousand years ago, Latin was the common language of the Roman Empire, which stretched from what is now Spain and England as far as Egypt and Iraq. Latin is the direct ancestor of many modern languages, including various Italian dialects, Spanish, Portuguese, French, Catalan, Occitan, Swiss Romansch, and Romanian.

In this session, students translate a two thousand-year-old poem by the poet Ovid (43 BCE–17/18 CE). In his youth, Ovid was a favorite of the Emperor Augustus, but at the age of fifty he was banished for saying something indiscreet in a poem. The poem used in the Poetry Inside Out program is "Metamorphoses," which tells about origins through changes of identity and body (the girl Daphne turns into a bay laurel tree). The three lines students are to focus on describe the chaos at the beginning of the universe, a subject dear to every fifth-grader's heart.

The most difficult part of translating Ovid is not the meaning of the words, but their relationship. Languages like English derive much of their meaning from syntax, the order of the words. In Latin, an adjective can be far from the noun it modifies, and the verb can come at the end of a long sentence.

Even with a full Translator's Glossary, students must struggle to rearrange the words. Their attempts are timid at first, modifying only a word or two, but inevitably, somebody gets bold (*Fortis fortuna adiuvat!*). Suddenly, for somebody, it clicks: *The sky which covers all!* Both the grammar and content of this poem invite students to think about how meaning is created—for words and humans—by relationships.

After translating Ovid, the students are asked to follow up on this theme by writing poems about the universe and/or about chaos. However, order is brought to the chaos by having the kids write in a pre-determined form: eleven lines of five words each, or eight lines of seven words each. Kids are fascinated by space, time, and larger cosmologies; they are delighted to tell us how the universe was born and where it is going.

Metamorphoses, Book 1, 5-7

Ovid, Latin (Ancient Rome)

Ante mare et terras et quod tegit omnia caelum
unus erat toto naturae vultus in orbe,
quem dixere chaos: rudis indigestaque moles

Before sea and land and sky which covers all,
there was whole of nature upon one entire circle,
which they called chaos: rough and confused trouble.

— Translation by Andrea Chen, 5th grade

Before sea and soil and sky which protects all glory
There was one entire territory face of nature
Which they called chaos: badly made,
    misarranged trouble.

— Translation by Wyattalless Greene, Jr., 4th grade

Misunderstood

Caroline María Woods-Mejía, 7th grade

In a sacred place, a creek is alive,
Shallow, murky, moving water.
A spider walks along the water.
"Look closely, follow our movements,"
the green water whispers.
A misplaced turtle bobs up and down,
swimming gracefully. Its striped shell and red head
floats near the surface and then disappears.
Ripples spread over and over again, like a
    never-ending secret.
A wilted tulip drifts by.
Water springs out creating unforgettable ripples.
And if you look closely, you can see
the copper glow of pennies, the creek
hopelessly misunderstood for a fountain.
Dead leaves drift upon the water.
The turtle observes this silently.
While the only spectator in the creek
is Abe Lincoln's copper face.

Original
Poems

Lonely

Elliot Zimmerman, 4th grade

Space and time were lonely
they created galaxies and black holes
Galaxies and black holes were lonely
they created planets and stars
Planets and stars were lonely
they made trees and flowers
Trees and flowers were lonely
they made animals and insects
Animals and insects were lonely
so they made many people
The people were never lonely

The Wind

Allie Allison, 11th grade

Is the wind obtainable?
It is always there, always around,
but untouchable.

Can the ocean and the wind
ever truly be close
and touch, connect?

As much as the ocean wishes it to be,
it will never occur.
It is forbidden.

They interact with one another,
the wind pushes the ocean causing great and mighty waves,
and the ocean accelerates the soft yet powerful breeze,
but they can never truly be together.

The wind is a fickle thing:
heading in one direction, then another,
never truly knowing what it wants.

The ocean: it is steady, swaying, moving
but it never lets focus or desire
slip from its grip.

So, by the natures of a different kind,
can they break the rules?

It is up to the wind and the wind alone,
for it is the only one that can make the decision.
The ocean has no say in the matter.

The ocean will be waiting, hoping, praying,
always ready for the wind to take it in its open arms.

If and when that beautiful time will ever come,
is a question that the
answer
is known.

Savili

Samoan translation by Asoiva Muasau of "The Wind"

E le savili, e savili mai lava
ma toe alu, ae le mafia ona
e tago lai.

E mafia e le sami ma le savili
ona fesoofai ae le mafia ona
tago iai.

I le tele o taimi o le sami, e le
mafia ona o'o i le auala e tapu
ai le fa'asalaga.

O lo'o feso'ota'i ma le isi tagata.
O'o le savili ma le sami e mafia
fesoota'i ile agi moi malü, e le
mafia ona fa'ateaogaira.

A'o le savili e agi mai pea o ia
e le magia ona motusia, se'i o'o
i le iuga mea uma.

I le savili e na'o ia lava le mafia
ona iai ma se isi lava mea.

O le sami e alu i luga ma tatalo,
toe sauniuni mo le matala le
alofa
deä.

The Dark Sky

like a huge
hole in the world
I see through my bedroom
window tiny stars
shining on
the dark sky

El cielo oscuro

como un gigante
hoyo en el mundo
yo veo por la ventana
de mi cuarto chiquitas
estrellas brillando en
el mundo oscuro

— Yésica Martínez López, 4th grade

Portal

Wipe the honey from my lips,
You who take the nectar of the flowers,
Wipe the salt off my brow,
And deliver me to the ocean,
Wipe the eyelash off my cheek,
And watch the wind carry me
Away.

— Lia Bruce, High School

The Edge

I walked through the white, wet clouds,
climbed up a thin branch, almost
       falling,
so I jumped back down
onto a fluffy cloud.
I kept on walking, wondering,
does this road go on for eternity?
While lost deep in my thoughts
a deer jumped out at me unexpectedly.
Rocks tumbled over, I had reached the
       edge.

    — Andrea Chen, 5th grade

The City

The city like a million icebergs in a polluted
ocean. The cracks like schools of fish.
The skyscrapers like an ocean volcano
going to erupt. The dazzling flowers
are corals dying. O how the city can be
the ocean or anything you can imagine.

    — Amiyo Cloarec, 5th grade

Journey

The women lay the bones
of her body on the bed
getting ready for
a great journey
under the sky
next to the salt water
with time
to collect beautiful seashells

— Kenya Milton, 6th grade

Family

The water I smell the laughter I
see my family having a barbecue
we come together and go into the
field and twirl in the grass me
and my sisters are in a circle
singing songs laughing having fun at night
we are still outside and we
are watching the stars in the sky

— Jamiah Owens, 4th grade

Session 15:
Ode to My Imagination

Already world-famous by the age of fifty, Pablo Neruda (Chile, 1904–1973) wrote three books of *Elemental Odes*, totaling some two hundred odes in all. The poems focus on common things: an artichoke, a tomato, salt, time, a book, a clock, the ocean. Neruda's odes drop down the page in thin lines—the reader's eye descends from image to image. An ode is a traditional praise poem, and to praise something is to give it close attention. Often, young poets, like Neruda, reach for extravagant figurative language to express their vision of ordinary things.

Also useful in illustrating odes for students is the book *Neighborhood Odes* by Chicano poet Gary Soto. Written in English, in frank imitation of Neruda's odes, but dedicated to childhood in a Mexican-American community, Soto's odes take on such common subjects as a sprinkler or tennis shoes. An ode can be written about absolutely anything, and this lesson is a time for students to hone their poetic tools.

Oda a la lagartija

Pablo Neruda, Spanish (Chile)

Junto a la arena
una
lagartija
de cola enarenada.
Debajo
de una hoja
su cabeza
de hoja.

De qué planeta
o brasa
fría y verde,
caíste?
De la luna?
Del más lejano frío?
O desde
la esmeralda
ascendieron tus colores
de una enredadera?

Del tronco
carcomido
eres vivísimo
retoño,
flecha
de su follaje.
En la piedra
eres piedra
con dos pequeños ojos
antiguos:
los ojos de la piedra.
Cerca
del agua
eres légamo taciturno
que resbala.
Cerca
de la mosca
eres el dardo
del dragón que
aniquila.

Y para mí,
la infancia,
la primavera
cerca
del río
perezoso,
eres
tú!
lagartija,
fría, pequeña
y verde:
eres una remota
siesta
cerca de la frescura,
con los libros cerrados.

El agua corre y canta.

El cielo, arriba, es una
corola calurosa.

Ode to a Lizard

Translation by Génesis Alejo and Gilberto Cuevas, 4th grade

Next to the sand
A
Lizard
With a tail of sand.
Under
A leaf
Its head
Of leaves.

From what planet
Or spark
Cold and green
Did you fall?
From the moon?
From the loneliest cold?
Or from
The emerald

Did your colors ascend
From a vine?

From the rotten
Vine
You are most alive
Sprout,
Arrow
From your foliage.
On the rock
You are
Rock
With tiny eyes
Ancient:
The eyes of the rock.
Close to the water
You are a silent ooze

That slips.
Close
To the fly
You are the dart
Of the dragon that kills.

And for my childhood,
The spring
Close
To the lazy
Lake,
It's
You!
Lizard
Cold and tiny
And green:
You are a remote nap

Close to the
    freshness
With books closed

The water runs
    and sings.

Up in the sky
There's a hot corolla.

Ode to My Life

My life has been
all about making jokes
Hiding my shame
I make people cheer up

Everyone but me

My only dream
came true twice
and the rest of my dreams
have gone.

— Salvador Centeno, 5th grade

Oda a la pelota

El sol en mis
manos la luna en
mis pies un limón
agrio que cuando
salta su jugo sale

Ode to My Ball

The sun on my
hand the moon on
my feet a sour
lemon when it jumps
its juice comes out

— Ricardo Antonio Espinoza, 4th grade

Oda a la imaginación

Alejandro Prieto, 4th Grade

Tu espacio profundo
callado como
la noche.
Una galaxia de sueños
sonando en tu cabeza
como una campana
en la misión.
Una luna de pensamientos
despertando
y durmiendo.
Unas estrellas
sentimentales
golpeando y jugando
riendo y chocando
toros corriendo,
sueños volando
en un hoyo oscuro.
Un sol despertando
una luna durmiendo
tomando turnos como
pescados comiendo.
La luz se
prende brillando.
Los niños
jugando.
Ese planeta
de inteligencia
resolviendo problemas
muy grandes
las luces
volando y
sumergiendo.

Ode to the Imagination

Translation by the Author

Your deep space
quiet like
the night.
A galaxy of dreams
sounding in your head
like a bell
in the mission.
A moon of thoughts
awakening
and sleeping.
Some sentimental
stars
hitting and playing
laughing and crashing
running bulls
flying dreams
in a black hole.
A sun awakening

a moon sleeping
taking turns like
fish eating.
The light
turns on glowing.
The kids
playing.
That planet
of intelligence
resolving problems
that are very big
the lights
fly and
sink.

— Alejandro Prieto, 4th grade

Bruno

Es como papel pura blanco
Corre rápido como un jaguar
Más flaco que un libro chico
Brinca fuerte como una rana
En la calle es rápido como águila
Muerde juguetes con dientes de metal
Come huesos como una vultura
Por chiquitos huecos se va

Bruno

He's like pure white paper
Runs as fast as a jaguar
Skinnier than a thin book
Jumps strong as a frog
Quick as an eagle in the street
Bites toys with metal teeth
Eats bones like a buzzard
Goes on through tiny hollows

— Oscar Antonio Sánchez, 4th grade

Ode to my Phone

It waits in my pocket
Scratched all over
A white line
On the back
From when it
Fell out my hand
Now it's night
My phone
Is playing jump-rope
With its charger
It goes to sleep
Just like me
My phone is important
It gets me connected
It's my friend so
If you see it
Don't touch it!!

Oda a mi teléfono

Me espera en mi bolsillo
Todo raspado
Una línea blanca
Por atrás
De cuando
Se cayó de mi mano
Ahora es de noche
Mi teléfono
Juega a saltar la cuerda
Con el cargador
Se duerme
Como yo
Mi teléfono es importante
Me conecta
Es mi amigo
Si lo ves ¡no lo toques!

— Karla Teleguario, 6th Grade

Oda a la flor

Una rosa como
un caballo
corriendo
la noche,
oscura bailarina,
bailando
con espinas
un corazón de fuego
una cara
que parece
muy enojada
fuego muy
caliente
como si una
casa se estuviera
quemando.
Fuego de sangre,
sangre en tu cuerpo.

Ode to the Flower

A rose like
a horse
running
the night,
dark ballerina,
dancing
with spikes
a heart of fire
a face
that looks
so mad
fire so
hot
as if a
house was
burning.
Fire of blood,
blood in our body.

— Lisa Maldonado, 4th grade

Steel and Darkness

Steel
and
darkness
the
incessant
whine
of
machines
whirling
in
automated
patterns
flashes
of
light
stars
and
galaxies
rushing
by
in
the
torn
earth
which
still
shakes
from
the
impact
of
the
train's
echoes

— Audrey Larkin, 11th grade

All This Could Happen

All This Could Happen

As they mature as writers across the course of a Poetry Inside Out residency, and as they learn from the masters whose work they translate and imitate, students become increasingly capable of employing advanced poetic forms in the service of their own vision. Once students have mastered shorter structures such as quatrains and tanka, they are able to put together more complex patterns, which channel their ideas into eloquent clarity. When they engage with traditional forms such as the sonnet, pantoum, and villanelle, PIO students are able to more fully realize their poetic potential, and when William Shakespeare (1564–1616) enters the classroom nothing is ever the same.

By this point in the program, students have developed their own critically wrought ideas about the uses of poetry. Héctor Collado (Panama, 1960–) and Taha Muhammad Ali (Palestine, 1931–) serve as points of departure for some of their most advanced work, as they take on the writing process itself with a critical eye, in poems about poetry: *metapoetics*.

Session 16: Poetic Forms Sonnets

The sonnet is a fourteen-line poem, usually rhymed. The sonnets of Shakespeare (1564–1616) use the rhyme scheme *abab//cdcd//efef//gg*. Since the Renaissance, sonnets have been written in hundreds of languages. The first sonneteer was most likely the Italian poet Francesco Petrarch (1304–74); some famous twentieth-century sonnet-writers include Edna St. Vincent Millay (1892–1950), Pablo Neruda (1904–1973), Octavio Paz (1914–1998), and Rainer Maria Rilke (1875–1926). Chinese sonneteer Zheng Min (1920–) writes:

> We were all fire birds—
> treading all our lives on red flames,
> threading through the hells. When bridges burned
> over our heads we never made a murmur ...

A traditional sonnet often turns between the eighth and ninth line, changing perspective. A problem may be set out in the first eight lines, to be solved in the last six. In the Shakespeare sonnet used in this PIO session, the poet spends the first eight lines complaining about his low self-esteem and lack of success; but in the last six lines, he remembers that he has a girlfriend, and becomes joyously happy. Fifth grade students can relate. PIO students learn to diagram rhyme schemes; our 14-line worksheet offers options of Shakespearean, Petrarchan, or unrhymed sonnets.

Sonnet XXIX

William Shakespeare, English (England)

When in disgrace with fortune and men's eyes,
I all alone beweep my outcast state
And trouble deaf heaven with my bootless cries
And look upon myself and curse my fate,
Wishing me like to one more rich in hope,
Featured like him, like him with friends possess'd,
Desiring this man's art and that man's scope,
With what I most enjoy contented least;

Yet in these thoughts myself almost despising,
Haply I think on thee, and then my state,
Like to the lark at break of day arising
From sullen earth, sings hymns at heaven's gate;
For thy sweet love remember'd such wealth brings
That then I scorn to change my state with kings.

Sonnet XXIX

Translated by Victor Qiu

When in misery about money and human perception
Alone I cry about my outcast state
And annoy deaf heaven with my useless cries
I look upon myself and curse my luck
Wish me a millionaire
I look like one, like him with his buddies
I like this man's drawings and that man's abilities
What I like is cool
In these thoughts I am reviled
Then I think about you and my fate
Like the bird that sings in the morning
From hell, angels sing carols at heaven's door
For your candy that money brings
I refuse to listen to the king's orders.

Sonnet XXIX

Translated by Keevan Tallon, 5th grade

When in misery because I have no money and people's perspectives
I isolated cry about my kicked-out state
I annoy the unlistening sky with my completely useless shouts
I look back on my past and swear on my future
I wish I had some hopeful hopenessy hope
I wish I looked like the cool guy in that movie
And I wish I could do what that guy can do
I'm not pleased

I almost hate me
I just happen to compare you and me and see my state
I'm like a birdie in da' morning
Earth is now sing'n songs
I just remembered I have a girl friend
And now I don't want to be an all-powerful space ninja!

If Time Were a Maze

Gracie Creed, 5th grade

If time were a maze
And universal monkeys bled
The world would be full of haze
Nothing would be unled

Nothing would be calm
Ducks could be called birds
You could see the world within your palm
They speak with little words

Books would be about rhyme
Something would be lost
Because of the words lost in time

And nothing would have a cost
Sunlight would become a single beam
All this could happen in a dream

Original
Poems

Cold Breezy Nights

Stacy Hu, 4th grade

Cold breezy nights are abandoned
Trees are lazily blowing in the crisp breeze
Branches are breaking off of oaks
Tsunamis are swimming to shore

Nature is in the bearing cold world
Winds are forming up in the pretty sky
Suns are beaming bright rays on earth
Imagination is swirling everywhere in your mind

Ships are bringing goods to places you've never visited
People are in lost forests, like being in mazes
Plants are growing in the Autumn

Rivers are ending at endless waterfalls
Clouds are raining puddles
But last, nothing is doing nothing at all.

Pantoums

Originally from Malaysia and popularized in the West by the French poet Victor Hugo (1802–1885), the pantoum is an interlocking form which repeats whole lines from stanza to stanza in the following pattern: *A-B-C-D // B-E-D-F // E-G-F-H // G-C-H-A*.

Four stanzas, four lines per stanza, sixteen lines in all, with each line repeated twice, means only eight different lines need to be written. But there are many possible outcomes to the arrangement of the lines, and the form encourages students to compose thoughtfully and revise creatively. The pantoum shuffles lines and frustrates narrative sequence, teaching students to craft modular phrases that reflect off of each other in different facets.

Hermanita

Kathy Espinoza, 4th grade

At five o'clock you will smile at me.
At midnight you will bloom like a rose.
At ten o'clock you will wake up and eat.
At eight o'clock you will cry a lot.

At midnight you will bloom like a rose.
I just can't explain how beautiful you are.
At eight o'clock you will cry a lot.
I hear you cry for about 25 minutes.

I just can't explain how beautiful you are.
You are just very incredible.
I hear you cry for about 25 minutes
But you are beautiful.

You are just very incredible.
At ten o'clock you will wake up and eat.
But you are beautiful.
At five o'clock you will smile at me.

la luna no ha bajado

Juan Daniel Pérez, 4th grade

no han encontrado al niño
cuando la luna no ha bajado
a las once estudiantes escuchan ruido
los trabajadores salen de su trabajo

cuando la luna no ha bajado
a las cinco los niños quieren salir
los trabajadores salen de su trabajo
todavía el cielo está brilloso

a las tres la escuela está trabajando
a la una los jóvenes juegan al fútbol
todavía el cielo está brilloso
cuando el sol se convierte en negro

a la una los jóvenes juegan al fútbol
a las once estudiantes escuchan ruido
cuando el sol se convierte en negro
no han encontrado al niño

the moon has not gone down

Translated by the Author

they still have not found the kid
when the moon has not gone down
at eleven the students hear noise
the workers finish their jobs

when the moon has not gone down
at five the kids want to go outside
the workers finish their jobs
the sky is still shining

at three the school is working
at one young people play soccer
the sky is still shining
when the sun turns black

at one young people play soccer
at eleven the students hear noise
when the sun turns black
they still have not found the kid

Campo y ciudad

Mario Pérez-Tell, 6th grade

¡Viva la tierra divina y gane la realidad!
Adoro los viejos bailes por el maíz,
    como luces tontas
mi campo tan bonito con mi corazón enterrado
maíz malo e inseguro, no saben hacer
    maíz seguro.

Adoro los viejos bailes por el maíz,
    como luces tontas
sustitutan mis ideas y las intentan
maíz malo e inseguro, no saben hacer
    maíz seguro
nuevos zapatapos blancos, unas buenas ideas.

Sustitutan mis ideas y las intentan
mis caballos galopean y zapateando también
nuevos zapatapos blancos, unas buenas ideas
un baile nuevo con inseguros que bailan.

Mis caballos galopean y zapateando también
mi campo tan bonito con mi corazón enterrado
un baile nuevo con inseguros que bailan
¡viva la tierra divina y gane la realidad!

Country and City

Translated by the Author

Hurray for the divine earth and reality wins!
I adore the old dances in the corn,
    like dumb lights
The nice field with my heart buried.
Bad corn and insane, they don't know
    how to make it.

I adore the old dances in the corn,
    like dumb lights
Substitute my ideas and they try it.
Bad corn and insane, they don't know
    how to make it.
New white tap-shoes, new ideas.

Substitute my ideas and they try it
My horses gallop and tap-dance too.
New white tap-shoes, new ideas.
A new dance with insecure people dancing.

My horses gallop and tap-dance too.
The nice field with my heart buried.
A new dance with insecure people dancing.
Hurray for the divine earth and reality wins!

Lines

Randell Rodríguez, 5th grade

Lines stretch on forever
For eternity and always
Everything baffles me
Nothing is understandable

For eternity and always
The wind will forever blow
Nothing is understandable
Time stops everything is frozen

The wind will forever blow
Non-stop and repeating itself
Time stops everything is frozen
The earth drowns in dark space

Non-stop and repeating itself
Everything baffles me
The earth drowns in dark space
Lines stretch on forever

Villanelles

The Villanelle is a nineteen-line poem with two repeating lines in the following pattern, where A and B are the repeating lines and X can be any line: *A-X-B // X-X-A // X-X-B // X-X-A // X-X-B // X-X-A-B*. The first known Villanelle was by Jean Passerat (France, 1534–1602), and the most famous villanelle is "Do not go gentle into that good night..." by Dylan Thomas (Wales, 1914–1953). Traditional villanelles rhyme, and though Poetry Inside Out students are encouraged to forgo the rhyme scheme to simplify this challenging form, Diego Piceno pulls off a rhymed villanelle as if it weren't hard at all.

Cyclops

Wyattalless Greene, Jr., 4th grade

Cyclops the one-eyed freak, big, tall and ugly
With heartshorts and a horn on his head
He always mess up making his bed

He's weird, fat, and so totally obnoxious
Wearing flip-flops, showing his crusty
   toes corny and green
Cyclops the one-eyed freak, big, tall and ugly

He eats hearts, plays darts and always
   gets a bullseye
His pet squid Ricardo loves to play all day
He always mess up making his bed

He eats rotten apples that has a face
   called death

His sister's name is Beth, she's a slob
   and eats glob
Cyclops the one-eyed freak, big, tall and ugly

He has a car, it's so dirty it makes pirates
   say scurvy
When he sleep it gives you the creeps
He always mess up making his bed

He loves thumbs, eats plums and sometimes
   his thumbs
Also pears with a side of bears
Cyclops the one-eyed freak, big, tall and ugly
He always mess up making his bed

If I Ever Reach You

Diego Piceno, 5th grade

If one day you will blow
tell me because I will say
if I ever reach you I'll let you know

it is time you must go
it is time it is today
if one day you will blow

I don't care, so
what if we go to the Bay
if I ever reach you I'll let you know

tell me again and I will show
I will show you the letter *jay*
if one day you will blow

I must care I need to go
now you leave or say
if I ever reach you I'll let you know

just go with the flow
today is the last day so play
if one day you will blow
if I ever reach you I'll let you know

Bears On the Inside

Sandra Zavala, 4th grade

We are all bears on the inside
We roam the snowy mountains
We swim through rivers and lakes

I wonder where do we all go
I bet we are going to unknown lands
We are all bears on the inside

We all are tired of the journey
When will we get there?
We swim through rivers and lakes

I wonder is this a dream
Or is it my reality?
We are all bears on the inside

We've gotten here
I feel the fresh air and I lie in the fresh water
We swim through rivers and lakes

I feel so free in the new land
What? Oh come on it was all a dream
We are all bears on the inside
We swim through rivers and lakes

Reach the Morning Sun

Saraí Castillo, 5th grade

I can reach for the stars
I can reach for the sky
But to reach the morning sun I take time

You have to listen You have to hear
You have to be so you can see
I can reach for the stars

Have I been a dream
Or have I been your moon
But to reach the morning sun I take time

I take a day to be with the sun
I take a night to be with the stars
I can reach for the stars

I have to dream to be alive
You have to breathe to be alive
But to reach the morning sun I take time

For you to reach the sun
You have to dream but
I can reach for the stars
But to reach the morning sun I take time

Question and Answer

Luis Tejeda, 5th grade

The clock moving like the wind
The wind moving the future
The future moving the people.

The people making cars, houses and
    other stuff
Soon there's going to be a lot of moving
But who's going to move the people?

Who's going to move the earth?
The question is God
But who's going to move God?

Nobody knows.
After they search, the answer is yourself.
We will replace the clocks.

We will replace the wind.
We will replace cars, houses and other stuff.
We will replace people.

We will move the earth.
We will move the searchers searching.
We will move the animals.
We will also move ourselves.

Session 17: Poems Should

As students make the process of translation and poetry their own, they naturally establish their own sense of priorities. They turn their critical and creative thinking, which they have learned from translating poems, onto poetry itself. Using the models put forth by the poets they have been translating, they are invited to write poems about poetry—this is called *metapoetics*.

Metapoetics helps to address the question of how student learning is assessed within PIO's immersion in poetry and translation. Students complete surveys prior to the PIO program, and then again at the end, but it is not always easy for them to explain their new understandings in critical prose, so they are encouraged to do it with poetry.

Taha Muhammad Ali (1931–) lost his home when his village was bombarded during the Israeli-Arab war of 1948. He left school after fourth grade but went on studying poetry on his own. For half a century he has run a souvenir shop near the Church of the Annunciation in Nazareth. Héctor Collado (1960–) is a notable children's poet and author from Panama.

Poema

Héctor Collado, Spanish (Panama)

Un poema no es un pájaro,
sino el vuelo de los pájaros.

No es la nube,
sino la canción de las nubes.

Un poema es una casa abierta,
con puertas y ventanas despiertas.

Un poema no es la flor,
sino el aroma de las flores.

No es un árbol,
sino el fruto de los árboles.

Un poema no es un verso,
sino el universo.

Poem

Translation by José Luis Moreno, 7th grade

A poem is not a dove,
rather the flight of the dove.

It is not the cloud,
rather the melody of the clouds.

A poem is an open house,
with windows and doors alert.

A poem is not a rose,
rather the scent of the rose.

It is not a tree,
rather the fruit of the tree.

A poem is not a verse,
rather the universe.

أَيْنَ؟

Taha Muhammad Ali, Arabic (Palestine)

اَلشِّعرُ يَكْمُنُ

في مَكانٍ ما

خَلْفَ لَيْلِ الكَلِماتِ

خَلْفَ غُيومِ السَّمَعِ

عَبْرَ عَتْمةِ البَصَرِ

وَراءَ غَسَقِ الموسيقَى

ما بَطَنَ مِنْها

وَما ظَهَرَ.

أَمّا أَيْنَ مَكْمَنُهُ؟

فَمِنْ أَيْنَ لي

أَنْ أَدْريَ أَيْنَ

وَأَنا لا أَكادُ أَعْرِفُ –

في عِزِّ نَهاري –

مَكْمَنَ قَلَمي أَيْنَ!

Where

Translated by Abdul Tawil, 5th grade

Poetry exists somewhere.
Behind the night of words.
Behind the clouds of sound.
Through the darkness of sight.
Behind the dusk of music,
the hidden and the known.
Where is its location?
How could I even tell
if I don't know at midday
where my pencil is!

Poetry

Poetry is written on paper.
Paper is made by people.
Nothing made people.
Nothing is not a thing.
Rain came from water.
Water came from the ocean.
The ocean came from the earth.
The earth is from a galaxy.
A galaxy is from space.
Space came from nothing.
The sky is full of clouds
and birds and rocks
and people and dogs.

— Johnny Xu, 4th grade

Original
Poems

Poesía

La poesía me tiene
encantada
Yo siento la sangre ardiente
la luz es la vida
de las personas
conozco muy
bien
el mundo

Poetry

Poetry has me
going crazy
I feel the burning fire
the light is life
of the people
I know the world
very
well

— Ashley Méndez, 4th grade

Poetry Inside Our Head

Poetry inside our head
the one I'm thinking of is
always perfectly written down
Poetry is ahead
heading and leading us
to the beautiful sun
Poetry is leading us to
see its sunset down
Down, down to the
lucky and muddy
garden with pretty flowers
and very green
grass. The sunset with
its beautiful ocean.

Poetry is behind my words
The words I'm writing are
all about my strongest poem
the one that I always
wanted to write
The words in the poem
are all about my own
life. My easy life of
all I wanted it to be
huge, strong and
lucky. Never on the word
I'm behind. Poem, poem,
will it be me once more?

— Elaine Wen, 5th grade

A Poem Is and Is Not

A poem is not the world
it's what happens in the world.

A poem is not water
but the entire ocean.

A poem is not a person's knowledge
but a flower's aroma.

A poem is not a plastic flower
but a real flower.

A poem is not a flower
but the honey in the rose.

A poem is not a beautiful rose
but a red-eyed tree-frog.

A poem is not the ground
but the smell of the dirt.

It's not a boat
but the wind in the sails.

A poem is not a tiger
but the stripes of the tiger.

— Anabeth De La Cruz, Barry Su, Sandra
Zavala, Janiah Owens, Chantel Larios,
Wyattalless Greene Jr., Saraí Castillo,
Lakeviona Adams, Zuleyma Márquez, 3rd
and 4th grades

Poems Should

A poem should be
the sound of running water.

A poem is a leaf falling off a tree
so it transforms into a dark star.

A poem should be as loud
as the Fourth of July.

A poem should be as
loud as a baseball game.

A poem should be as quiet
as the library.

A poem should be as
quiet as the air.

Un poema debe ser escrito
en la tierra silenciosa.

A poem should be written
in the silent earth.

Poems should rhyme like
Dr. Seuss did in *A Cat In a Hat*.

Poems should tell reality of your life
no fake thing.

A poem should be like a tornado
snatching words from people.

A poem should be with rage to make
all the pain go away on the inside.

A poem ripped my finger off
for no reason I wonder why.

Poetry should fly like a dragon
breathing fire out its mouth.

Poems should bring down the sun
like water brings down the sun.

A poem should be our spirits
A poem should be our lives

A poem should
take its words out to dinner.

Poems should have money
or am I just dreaming.

— Alexus Smith, Rigoberto Bañuelos,
   Adán García, Christian Moreno,
   Jermaine Robinson, Mark Sombra,
   Gaby Martínez, Kimberly Espinoza,
   Amani Tahsen, Anabeth De La Cruz,
   Gerardo González, Wyattalless
   Greene Jr., Jesús Garduño,
   Senait Barber-Ainsworth, Ivan
   Zamora, Luis Tejeda, Darshaya
   Washington, Lakeviona Adams,
   3rd, 4th and 5th grades

Nuts and Bolts

Nuts and Bolts

A summary of poems and curriculum ideas doesn't fully describe the procedures, practices, and experience that make up a Poetry Inside Out residency. In this final section, we offer a field guide to revising and improving original poems, followed by some examples of students' own poem-pages, developed for school anthologies. Observer Cheryl Rodby provides a fascinating perespective on students' actual day-to-day classroom experience of Poetry Inside Out, while Audrey Larkin, who began translating and writing poetry with PIO in fourth grade and is now a senior in high school, discusses how the program changed her life. Finally, we have collated a series of PIO Best Practices that we have found to work in a residency setting.

Revision and Publication

Revision is more than copy-editing and correcting spelling—within the Poetry Inside Out program, revision is cast as *re-vision*, seeing anew. As the PIO residency draws to a close, students revisit the poems and translations they wrote over the course of the semester, and with time having passed, they are able to look at them more objectively and make changes.

The kids are given a Revision Checklist that provides basic procedures for the practice of revision and editing. They are lead through the procedure, often with a volunteer willing to have her poem critically examined by the group. The author is reminded that it's still his or her poem, and s/he is always free to accept or reject the class's suggestions.

Here, sixth-grader Vy Huynh systematically discovers more creative and less expected word choices en route to revising the poem from the "River of Self" exercise (Session 12).

Star

Vy Huynh, 6th grade

Voila. I have become a star.
This will be a great adventure in the sky.
What shall they call me?
Where did this bright light come from?
What secrets will I ~~discover~~?
What joy? What pain? What greatness?

My apologies to all the ~~geographers~~.
I didn't ~~mean~~ to do this.
I just love to look at the stars upon the sky.
There are many ~~great people~~ in the world.
It is for them that I became a star.

I never like to see ~~hidden faces~~ being a
star, who knows, I could ~~hide~~ instead.

I never like to see ~~sky~~
being a star. I could cover instead.
My destiny may then be to shine out all
shyness ~~to the sun.~~

Star

Voila. I have become a star.
This will be a great adventure in the sky.
What shall they call me?
Where did this bright light come from?
What secrets will I seek?
What joy? What pain? What greatness?

My apologies to all the astronomers.
I didn't do this on purpose.
I just love to look at the stars upon the sky.
There are many closets in the world.
It is for them that I became a star.

I never like to see shyness shine being a
star, who knows, I could shine instead.

I never like to see darkness cover
being a star. I could cover instead.
My destiny may then be to shine out all
shyness and darkness from the earth.

Student Poem-Pages

From its inception, Poetry Inside Out has used poem-pages to present the model master poems for students to translate. Each poem-page typically contains, along with the model poem, a photo of the poet, a paragraph biography, and a translator's glossary of key words that may present difficulties. As we approach the publication deadline for our student anthology, it is a thrilling exercise for the students to design their own poem-pages, which may include a self-portrait or a translation of their poem.

Sydneé Blackwell

San Francisco, CA

Street Livers

A sweet dream can be a beautiful nightmare.
Well, at least that's what I used to hear.
You never hear these things any more cause all the
    positives turn to negatives.
When us Colors go shoot craps on corners
and sell our bodies on E14
and drink Bacardi at little kids' birthday parties.

When I try to ask,
"Do you do this for a living?"
I get no response.
"Why is that?" I ask myself.
Why would you turn down the opportunity of
    getting help?

It's like running away from a new life being rel
    when you know
it's goanna have to happen someday.
And once that seed is planted there's
    no shovel to dig it back up.
And the sun is shining.
And the water is being poured.
And that seed deserves a chance to grow.
And just because your seed didn't grow
    doesn't mean this seed has to suffer.
Street livers, why? I mean why?
Why do this to your young selves?
They say, "Have you ever been mistreated
    so badly at home where you get socked and

My name is Sydneé Blackwell. I am twelve years old. I am from San Francisco. Once I came in second place in a school team poetry slam. I hope to be able to get a full scholarship to college to play basketball.

socked in the chest for every petty thing
    and the only way to make you feel
    even is to torture your life?"
So when you return, you don't have to take
    your anger out on them?"

TURN THE LIGHTS ON.

All these young people stuck in ditches that
    not one little shovel can dig them out.
Not even a bulldozer.
They never get a chance to see the light cuz
    their life ends while they're in the dark

Street Livers.

Translator's Glossary

Anger (v): Enojar
Bulldozer (n): Una máquina excavadora
Bodies (n): Cuerpos
Dig (v) as in dig them out: Desenterrarla
Hear (v): Oír, oyes—you hear
Livers (n): A person that that lives in the street;
    Viviradores, habitantes
Mistreated (v): Maltratado
Opportunity (n): Oportunidad
Reborn (v): Renacer
Running (v): Correr
Socked (v): Puñetazo
Sweet (adj.): Dulce
Young people (n); Jovenes

Génesis Alejandra Alejo Delval

Génesis Alejandra Alejo Delval nació en Oakland. Su familia es de Cotoclán, Jalisco. Hablan español en casa. Le gusta irse a visitar a unos ranchos. Lo que le hace más feliz es su primita que tiene ocho meses, Angela Celeste.

Empty Mind

My mind is empty with no ideas
I think …. think … but nothing
Nothing that is nothing at all
I only think of chocolate!

I think …. think … but nothing
I'm just wondering for ideas!
I only think of chocolate!
My mind is thinking with its mind.

I'm just wondering for ideas!
The clock is wasting time
My mind is thinking with its mind.
earth has to stop so I can think

The clock is wasting time
Nothing that is nothing at all
earth has to stop so I can think
My mind is empty with no ideas

Mente vacía

Mi mente está vacía sin ideas
Pienso, pienso, pero nada
Nada que es nada
¡Solo pienso en chocolate!

Pienso, pienso, pero nada
No más estoy buscando ideas
¡Solo pienso en chocolate!
Mi mente está pensando con su mente

No más estoy buscando ideas
El reloj está gastando tiempo
Mi mente está pensando con su mente
el mundo debe parar para que piense

El reloj está gastando tiempo
Nada que es nada
el mundo debe parar para que piense
Mi mente está vacía sin ideas

A Fly on the Classroom Wall

Cheryl Rodby

Cheryl Rodby, a retired Oakland school principal, observed the sequence of several Poetry Inside Out residencies in spring 2010. Her detailed classroom observations convey the feeling and process of what goes on as the children struggle at first with unfamiliar concepts and then begin to master the processes of poetry and translation. Here is a selection of her observations:

Session 2

"The instructor was explaining how a phrase is sometimes different in English than in Spanish. He asked a small group of students how they would say that a person knew a whole poem without looking at the book. One child said 'memorize.' The instructor then touched his heart and Luana said, 'They would know it by heart!'"

Session 3

"One young man appeared to be struggling at first. Then all of a sudden he said, 'Oh, I get it!' and he took off translating the rest of the poem. It was as if you could see the light bulb go off in his head. He was very pleased with himself and appeared to enjoy the rest of the assignment."

Session 5

"A few of the students take the words too literally. They may know one meaning for a word and they want to make it fit or they don't want to use the word. One girl asked about the word 'remote.' 'Isn't that what you use to change the channel on the television?' The classroom teacher explained that a word can have more than one meaning, and in this poem 'remote' means far away. The student struggled with this idea as she wrote her original poem. She kept wanting the teacher to reassure her that she was 'right.' There is that concept again... right and wrong."

Session 6

"With little direction this fourth-grade class is able to translate poetry and create their own original poems using some of the more interesting words from the translated poem. They haven't however been able to allow themselves to find that balance where their thoughts and words flow freely without worrying about whether what they are writing is right or wrong or makes sense. There are a few exceptions... This will be a good group to explore the question the instructor raised yesterday about what are the parts of the foundation we have built over the weeks with these students that gives them the self confidence in their own writing of poetry to find that balance where creativity takes over."

Session 8

"Then it happened! a magical, miracle 'aha' moment! When the instructor asked the students to share their translation of the third line and one child nailed it, stating 'I get it, it's about translating in an order and meaning that makes sense,' most of the students seemed to get it."

Session 10

"It was very powerful when the instructor talked about how your mind works when you write poetry, stating that you don't think about what is right or wrong, you just let the words and ideas flow. He went on to describe how they can find a balance between chaos and order in writing. Within that balance is where creativity happens. He put a few words on the board such as nothing, chaos, universe, and the students came up with other words such as rain, year, lost, found, sadness and forgetting. There was a breakthrough for this class today. Most of the students allowed their thoughts to flow which allowed their creativity to shine through. They are beginning to find that balance between chaos and order in their writing."

Session 12

"There were three 'aha' moments in the classes today. The first came when third-grader Josiah dictated a pantoum to the instructor, who took the time to write all of his words down on paper for him. This was the first poem he ever created for this class. He then went on to write a second pantoum on his own. Yeah Josiah!!!!

The next 'aha' moment also came in the third grade after Destiny completed her pantoum. She announced, 'I'm done.' Another student, Mark, said 'Sir, isn't it true that you are never done in poetry?'

The third 'aha' moment was something many teachers wait their whole career hoping to see. Students in the fifth-grade class were actually disappointed that the recess bell rang and interrupted their work. They cheered when they were told they could keep working on their pantoums and have recess later."

A PIO Student's Story

Audrey Larkin

I never expected my lower-level fourth-grade Spanish class to have a spectacular influence on my life. As a girl coming from a monolingual, English-speaking family, who had started my school's Spanish immersion program a year late, this somewhat remedial placement was hardly unexpected, if not wholly appreciated. Little did I know that this class would be lucky enough to get a Poetry Inside Out residency, and that years later I would shudder to think about what would have happened if my Spanish had been just a bit better.

In this class I was introduced to poetry, literary translation, and what it truly means to be bilingual. My teacher, Michael P. Ray, who worked as part of Poetry Inside Out, a program sponsored by the Center for the Art of Translation, asked the class to translate great Spanish poets such as Pablo Neruda, Octavio Paz, and José Martí from Spanish to English. Literary translation, as I soon found out and continually rediscover, is terribly difficult. To translate a poem one must first understand a highly complex work of art well enough to exactly transpose its meaning into another language. One must delve into the mind of an extremely gifted writer and see the poem through the poet's eyes. But that is just half the work. To translate a poem well, one must also have a remarkable sense of two languages, of their nuances, their wordplay, their flow, their sounds, and the subtle difference between synonyms. In brief, especially for a girl still learning Spanish, it was, and is, a thankless task, because no matter how much one works, edits, tweaks, and shuffles through a Spanish-English dictionary, the poem simply sounds better in the original language. Still, in the process of translation, one comes to know a poem so well, so intimately, as each word is pondered, considered, and wrestled with, that a little bit of the author's brilliance is rubbed into the translator, and one understands, even if it is unconsciously, something more about language and poetry. It is inevitable. Thus, through the process of translation, I was introduced to poetry.

However, not only did I translate poems, but Michael Ray had us write poetry as well. We translated great poets, and then wrote poems inspired by their work. This was my favorite part of class. To me, poetry has always been a form of self-expression. In fourth grade I wrote about rabbits, the sun, and fall leaves, but all these objects ultimately served as metaphors that became irrevocably tangled up in my experiences and emotions. Even now, it is the same way. Often, I have felt that I am most honest in my poetry. For me poetry is very personal, but also strangely universal. It is a way of mixing up language and arranging words in a different, new, and beautiful way. It is another way of thinking, of casting familiar objects in a distinct light, of playing and luxuriating in language. I have continued to work with Poetry Inside Out ever since that fourth-grade class, and the wonder and enjoyment of writing poetry has grown in me ever since.

I must admit that there are days when writing a poem seems like an impossible task, and putting pencil marks on paper is a Herculean feat. There are days when I angrily cross out all the lines of a poem in disgust, but can't think of anything to replace them with. There are days when, even after ten years of studying the language, my Spanish makes me cringe, when all Spanish speakers seem to be speaking at the speed of light, when I forget simple phrases, get flustered and make a complete fool of myself. But there are other days when I write easily and naturally, driven just by the pleasure of creating poetry. There are days when I think and even dream in Spanish.

Slowly, I'm learning.

Poetry Inside Out
Best Practices

Poetry Inside Out Curricula

Spanish Curriculum

PIO's traditional Spanish curriculum, developed through constant teaching practice since 2000, consists of over 350 poem-pages representing a vast range of Spanish-speaking countries.

Chinese Curriculum

Development of PIO's Chinese curriculum began in 2009. Drawn from the long and rich tradition of Chinese-language poetry, this curriculum introduces students to a variety of works, from ancient times up to the present day. Students flex their cognitive and creative muscles as they engage different forms of Chinese language written in different times and places.

World Poetry Curriculum

PIO's World Poetry curriculum, developed since 2008, now has poem-pages representing nineteen different languages, along with translator's glossaries that help students translate from languages they may not know.

Poem-Pages

We present all our model poems via poem-pages, which generally include the text in the original language, a translator's glossary, a picture of the poet, and his or her biography. The poem-page is central to PIO instruction. Students are encouraged to create their own personal poem-pages at the end of a workshop for inclusion in the school anthology.

Translator's Glossary

Every poem-page comes equipped with a translator's glossary. Typically these focus on a few words which present particularly interesting difficulties, offering a definition and a range of English synonyms. In situations where the students may not speak the language, the glossary may define every single word in the poem.

Translation Circles

In translation circles, students work in groups of four, with as much mixed language expertise as possible. Student volunteers read the poem aloud to the whole class. Ideally, this includes at least one native speaker to read the poem in the original language. Once the poem has been read aloud several times, and each member of the group has read the poem silently, the group discusses the content of the poem.

The groups of four then break into pairs for phrase-by-phrase rough translations. This can be done using the translator's glossary and a bilingual dictionary, if necessary. Once the phrase-by-phrase translation is complete the groups re-form, and students share their rough translations, with each pair making changes based on what they learn from the other pair. As a group, the students discuss possible interpretations, words or phrases that were particularly difficult to translate, and which words were most interesting. Groups then rejoin for whole class discussion, having picked three examples of things that were interesting or difficult to translate to share with the class.

Sessions

The standard PIO residency consists of sixteen sessions with a visiting poet-translator who functions as a teaching artist. The program-dissemination workshops have varying schedules to fit the needs of partner institutions; a classroom teacher, certified in our workshops, may choose to schedule PIO lessons throughout the year. We think of a session as a classroom hour, which is usually about 50 minutes but will go deeper with 75. You may well choose to teach what we call a Session in two separate class periods, one for translating a text and the next for composing an original poem.

Worksheets

PIO students write their poems on worksheets formatted to help them make the transition from translation to original poetry. "It is so much easier for kids to deal with the quatrain assignment than to pour their thoughts unstructured onto a blank page," writes classroom assistant Molly Wheeler. "When they see the blank spaces for them to fill in with words on their worksheet, it makes them feel like the poem already exists; they just have to find it."

Revision Checklist

- Choose your best/favorite poem. Read it to yourself silently: how does it sound? Does it make sense?

- Edit: take out any unnecessary words or verses, especially; "a, the, then, next, after, because, like, and..." Change boring, tired words into more interesting, exciting words. Use a thesaurus.

- Add more detail, more richness. Maybe your poem needs to be longer.

- Especially if your poem forms a series of somewhat independent stanzas, like a set of haiku or Guess the Color, you may want to arrange them in a new order.

- Where is your poem's true beginning? Where is its ending? Maybe your poem needs to be shorter. Maybe you thought you were writing one long poem and it is really two short ones.

- Share your poem with a partner. Make suggestions to each other to help improve your poems. Read it again: does it sound better?

- Correct mistakes.

- Translate your poem into another language or trade with a partner and translate each other's poem.

School Anthologies

Every Poetry Inside Out residency or workshop produces an anthology of student translations and poems, which includes every participant, and then each student receives a copy. Students choose their own poem(s) in mono- or bilingual format, write a bio, draw a self-portrait, or pose for the camera. The last page of each anthology is always reserved for autographs and dedications so that the poets can inscribe their published work to each other.

Professional Development

In addition to our residencies taught by poet-translators, Poetry Inside Out offers a professional development program, which trains school staff to implement the PIO curriculum on their own. PIO also does poetry and translation workshops for cultural institutions that complement programs and exhibits.

River of Words

Caroline María Woods-Mejía's poem "Misunderstood" won a $100 Grand Prize in the 2009 Creekseekers poetry competition, judged by former Poet Laureate Robert Hass and sponsored by River of Words and the San Francisco Estuary Coalition. Four other PIO students were finalists. In the last seven years, PIO has placed 33 finalists and PIO students have won four Grand Prizes in River of Words' annual contests for the best environmental and nature art and poetry.

Poetry Inside Out Across Grade Levels

You will notice that these lessons and exercises aren't divided according to grade level. In fact, all of these writing ideas can and have been used successfully with students at many levels, ranging from elementary school through middle school, high school and even college. Given patience and willing hands to take dictation, some of these poems can be adapted to first- or second-graders, but generally PIO workshops are not offered below the third grade. An exercise that takes one classroom hour in fifth grade may take two hours for third-graders. Fourth- through sixth-graders have an avid interest in wordplay and are ready to take on surprisingly complex assignments. In middle school, students' focus often shifts to themes of personal identity and social justice. High school students have more years of "coloring within the lines" to unlearn, and they may take longer to embrace the empowerment of divergent possibilities.

Poetry Inside Out: Easy or Hard?

Early on, as kids work through the first few relatively straightforward exercises in the PIO program, they often complain about the difficulty of the assignments. The majority of their first translations tend to be tentative, unadventurous, word-for-word, literal translations that stick so close to the original text that they may not make sense in English. Their early original poems may satisfy the assignment to the letter, but don't go much further. At this point, the children don't seem to know what right answer we're looking for, and they experience the processes of translation and poetry writing as painstakingly difficult.

And then, along about the middle of the residency, in the words of observer Cheryl Rodby, "the light-bulb goes on." The kids are surprised to find that we were looking for something simpler and deeper than they expected. Student writing begins to move of its own accord, as each classroom develops its own subculture of poetry writing. At the end of their PIO experience, fourth and fifth-grade classes were asked to identify their best poem, and to comment on whether writing it had been easy or hard. 79% said writing their best poem was Easy; just 9% said Hard, while 12% were Not Sure.

A sampling of student comments:

The poem just came to my mind...
It was easy because I use my imagination or something
  goes right through me...
It was easy, like I already had all the ideas, flowing...
My best poem was easy to write because all the
  words came to my mind...
I just thought about the rain and how it would fall
  to the ground...
Easy, because I used sounds and my dreams...
It was hard to think of but after a few minutes it
  popped into my head...
I always think of words and I let myself go...
It just blasted out of me.

Clearly, something profound happens as kids use transla-tion to become poets. Perhaps this process is analogous to what Betty Edwards, author of the eponymous course of drawing exercises, calls "Drawing On the Right Side of the Brain." Long and often frustrating work has prepared these students to enter a zone where there is a different right answer for each person. Writing poetry, even in advanced traditional forms, becomes an almost effortless activity.

Biographies

Rafael Alberti was a member of the renowned, Spanish "Generation of '27" and a friend of the poets Federico García Lorca and Pablo Neruda. Because of his opposition to the fascist government that took over after the Spanish Civil War, Alberti had to live in exile, first in Argentina and later in Italy, for 39 years.

María Luisa Artecona de Thompson is a poet, teacher, fiction-writer, and playwright, who was awarded the Premio Doncel for Children's Literature in 1965. Her writing has been published in anthologies in Paraguay and abroad.

Matsuo Basho was a famous poet of the Edo period of Japan (1608–1868) and is the most renowned haiku poet of all time. He went simply by Basho, which means "plantain." His "frog haiku," written in 1686, has been translated hundreds (if not thousands) of times into dozens of languages.

Héctor Collado was born in Panama City, Panama, and writes poetry and fiction. His collections *De trompos y rayuelas* (Hopscotch and Tops) and *¡Kakirikakiri!* were awarded the national Medio Pollito prize for children's literature. He founded and directs the José Martí poetry workshop.

Haitian exile **René Depestre** is known throughout the world for his poetry, prose, and social commentaries, as well as for working side by side with prominent contemporaries such as Alejo Carpentier, Nicolás Guillén, and Pablo Neruda. Depestre published his first book of poetry in 1945, at the age of nineteen. He refuses to return to his native Haiti because, in his opinion, Haiti has become a zombie, a "violent contrast" to the Haiti he knew and loved while growing up in the port town of Jacmel.

Alfredo Espino, from El Salvador, is best known for his nature poems. After his parents forbade him to marry his girlfriend, he drowned his sorrows in the red-light district of San Salvador, and committed suicide at twenty-eight. "El nido," one of his most famous poems, comes from his book *Jícaras tristes* (Sad Gourds), which was published posthumously.

David Huerta was inspired to become a poet when he was a child watching his father, the well-known poet Efraín Huerta, draw pictures and construct poems. He has gone on to publish numerous collections of poetry, including *Before Saying Any of the Great Words: Selected Poems* (Copper Canyon, 2009), translated by Mark Schafer. Huerta has also translated work from Italian and English into Spanish, works as an editor at Fondo de Cultura Económica, and teaches literature at the Universidad Autónoma de México.

Audrey Larkin began translating and writing poetry in 2003 when she was in the fourth grade. She worked with Poetry Inside Out through middle school, and won a Grand Prize in the national River of Words contest as a seventh-grader she was flown with her family to Washington, D.C. to read her poem at the Library of Congress. She spent her junior year of high school as an exchange student in Zaragoza, Spain.

Jorge Luján was born in Córdoba, Argentina, and studied architecture. By chance he was in Lima, Perú, in March, 1976, when the Argentine military took power and disappeared more than 30,000 people. Luján quit architecture and became a poet and musician. He has lived for thirty years in Mexico City, and performs at musical events and *espectáculos*, records CD's and writes books of poetry for children. He teaches poetry at La Escuela Williams.

Taha Muhammad Ali's village was destroyed in the Arab-Israeli war of 1948, and his formal education ended after the fourth grade, but he continued to study poetry. For over fifty years, he has supported his family by selling souvenirs from his shop near the Church of the Annunciation in Nazareth. He has published four books of poetry in Arabic and a volume of short stories. His selected poems in English, *So What*, translated by Peter Cole, Yahya Hijazi, and Gabriel Levin, was published by Copper Canyon in 2006.

Pablo Neruda was born July 12, 1904, in Parral, Chile, as Eliecer Neftalí Ricardo Reyes Basualto, and brought up from age six in the small city of Temuco. The Nobel Prize laureate credited the mystical landscape of the South of Chile with developing his poetic consciousness. His pseudonym comes from the name of a Czech symbolist poet, which he took to avoid the wrath of his father, a railroad conductor, who had no use for poetry. In his late book *Libro de Preguntas* (*Book of Questions*) he asks:

> Is anything stupider in the world
> than to name oneself Pablo Neruda?

Ovid was born in 43 BCE to a wealthy family in Sulmo, a town near Rome. While still a teenager he disappointed his father by abandoning the study of law to become a poet. His most famous work is the Metamorphoses, an epic poem fifteen books long, which describes the creation and history of the universe in terms of Greek myths. When he was 51, Ovid was exiled by the emperor Augustus, and sent to live in the lonely village of Tomis on the far-away Black Sea.

Salvatore Quasimodo was born in Modica, Sicily. When he was seven years old, his family moved to Messina so that his father could help the victims of a devastating earthquake. Salvatore published his first poems when he was sixteen. Along with Giuseppe Ungaretti and Eugenio Montale, he is considered one of the foremost Italian poets of the 20th century. Winner of the Nobel Prize for Literature in 1959, Quasimodo was also an accomplished translator of Greek poetry.

Widely considered the greatest poet who ever lived, and certainly the greatest in the English language, William

Shakespeare is credited with authoring more than thirty plays. The sonnet in this volume is from his sequence of 154 sonnets, written around the turn of the century but not published until 1609.

At age 26, **Tawara Machi** took Japan by storm with the publication of her first work: a book of tanka entitled *Sarada kinenbi*, (*Salad Anniversary*). She became an overnight celebrity. Readers inspired by Tawara's poems have sent her tens of thousands of letters, and with them well over 200,000 tanka, over a thousand of which she has compiled and published. The oldest contributor is a 91-year-old man; the youngest an eleven year-old girl. Tawara is also a well-known translator of Japanese classical literature into contemporary Japanese.

Rominka Vet is one of the Mayan women who works with Taller Leñateros, an indigenous printing collective in San Cristóbal de Las Casas, in the southern Mexican state of Chiapas. A collection of the spells, incantations, and drinking songs of the Mayan women, *Conjuros y ebriedades*, is available as *Incantations*, a Spanish-English bi-lingual edition from Cinco Puntos Press (www.cincopuntospress.com).

Xi Xi is the pen-name of Zhang Yan. Born in Shanghai to Cantonese parents during the Japanese occupation, Xi Xi moved to Hong Kong with her family in 1950. Xi Xi started submitting her poems to magazines and newspapers while still in junior high school, and while in high school she published a sonnet. She later branched out from poetry to fiction, children's stories, translations, reviews, and experimental films. Retired from teaching, she remains active as a writer.

Index *by Student*

Index *by School*

Credits

Rafael Alberti, Stanzas from the poems "Rojo", "Azul", "Blanco", "Verde", "Negro", and "Amarillo" from the work *A la pintura*. Copyright © Rafael Alberti, 1948. El alba del alhelí, S.L.

Taha Muhammad Ali, "Where" from *So What: New & Selected Poems 1971–2005*, translated by Peter Cole, Yahya Hijazi, and Gabriel Levin. Original Arabic copyright © 2006 by Taha Muhammad Ali. Reprinted with the permission of Copper Canyon Press, www.coppercanyon.org

René Depestre, "La rivière" from *Hadriana dans tous mes rêves* copyright © Gallimard. Used with permission.

Pablo Neruda, "Oda a la lagartija" from *Nuevo sodas elementales* copyright © Fundacion Pablo Neruda, 2010. Used with permission.

Salvatore Quasimodo, "ed è subito sera" copyright © Arnoldo Mondadori Editore S.p.A., Milano. Used with permission.

Rominka Vet, "Bolom chon" from *Conjuros y ebriedades*, translated by Ambar Past copyright © 1998; and from *Incantations* copyright © 2005 and 2009. Reprinted with the permission of Ambar Past and Cinco Puntos Press.

Acknowledgments

Poetry Inside Out is supported by grants from the Walter & Elise Haas Fund, The San Francisco Foundation, the Fleishhacker Foundation, the Stocker Foundation, Amazon.com, and the National Endowment for the Arts. The editors wish to thank the entire staff and board of the Center for the Art of Translation for their support, and Anita Sagástegui, who introduced much new poetic material to the Poetry Inside Out curriculum.

Thanks also to all the teachers, principals, interested parents, and school personnel who have helped make Poetry Inside Out a success:

Cynthia Ashley
Monique Armstrong
Melissa Barnes-Dholakia
Luby Becerra
Oscar Bermeo
Carolyn Bice

Mina Bravo
Jeff Brennecke
Melanie Broder
Jeannie Bruland
Ella Bustamente
Pauline Chávez
Jamaal Clarke
Carmen Denhams
Maggie Engelsbe
Licita Fernández
Barbara Flannery
Marco Franco
Patrick Galleguillos
Xochitl García
Amelia Glaber
Brianna Goodman
Paula Guzmán
Tina Hernández

Teri Hudson
Richard Illig
Alex Janvelian
Joanna Jorfald
Autumn King
Jerome Kuo
Brian Lamb
Athena Larios
Laurette Lau
Emily Lee
Ceci Lewis
Gilberta Maldonado
Cecilia Melgare
Valerie Miner
Tina Morris
Rachel Nichols
John Pluecker
Andrew Poon
Michael P. Ray
Clarié Rodríguez

Carlyn Scheinfeld
Ben Seay
Lacey Shimizu
Jenna Stauffer
Melanie Swanby
Theresa Tam
Josephine Tang
Max Tarcher
Debra Taylor
Linda Twichell
Laura Urquiaga
Priscilla Vásquez
Nadine Wassef
Christine Wenrich
Andrew Whitworth
Kathy Wilson
Alexander Zwissler

About Poetry Inside Out

Since 2000, Poetry Inside Out has fostered imagination and built students' problem solving, critical thinking, and literacy skills through the translation and composition of poetry. Working with accredited teachers and professional poet-translators, Poetry Inside Out students are given the tools that enable them to translate work by the world's great poets. Students delve into the words, lines, cadences, and structure of a poem as they become inspired, capable, and adventurous enough to compose their own creative works.

Poetry Inside Out is a program of the Center for the Art of Translation, a non-profit organization that broadens cultural understanding through international literature and translation, working in publishing, teaching, and public events. In addition to Poetry Inside Out, the Center makes global voices and great literature accessible to individuals and communities through the two lines anthologies of world writing in translation and Two Voices, a reading series featuring international authors and translators.

Join Us

As a non-profit education program, Poetry Inside Out relies on readers and teachers like you to help support our efforts to share the importance of translation as a vital bridge between languages and people. Please consider making a donation to the Center. Find out more or make a pledge at www.catranslation.org.

Autographs